新丝路"中文+职业技能"系列教材委员会
（中文+机电一体化）

总策划：马箭飞　谢永华
策　划：宋永波　孙雁飞
顾　问：朱志平（北京师范大学）
　　　　林秀琴（首都师范大学）
　　　　宋继华（北京师范大学）

总主编：谢永华　杜曾慧
语言类主编：严　峻
专业类主编：芮红艳
语言类副主编：陆　杨　余　音
专业类副主编：杨海波　甄久军　徐　峰

项目组长：郭风岚
项目副组长：付彦白
项目成员：郭　冰　武传霞　齐　琰　赫　栗　李金梅

 新丝路"中文+职业技能"系列教材
New Silk Road "Chinese + Vocational Skills" Series

中文+机电一体化
Chinese + Mechatronics

初级 Elementary

新丝路"中文+职业技能"系列教材编写委员会 编

© 2023 北京语言大学出版社，社图号 23112

图书在版编目（CIP）数据

中文 + 机电一体化 . 初级 ／ 新丝路"中文 + 职业技能"系列教材编写委员会编 . -- 北京：北京语言大学出版社，2023.10（2024.1重印）

新丝路"中文 + 职业技能"系列教材
ISBN 978-7-5619-6333-3

Ⅰ. ①中… Ⅱ. ①新… Ⅲ. ①汉语－对外汉语教学－教材 ②机电一体化－教材 Ⅳ. ① H195.4 ② TH-39

中国国家版本馆 CIP 数据核字（2023）第 161689 号

中文 + 机电一体化（初级）
ZHONGWEN + JIDIAN YITIHUA (CHUJI)

排版制作： 北京创艺涵文化发展有限公司
责任印制： 周 燚

出版发行： 北京语言大学出版社
社　　址： 北京市海淀区学院路 15 号，100083
网　　址： www.blcup.com
电子信箱： service@blcup.com
电　　话： 编 辑 部 8610-82303647/3592/3395
　　　　　　国内发行 8610-82303650/3591/3648
　　　　　　海外发行 8610-82303365/3080/3668
　　　　　　北语书店 8610-82303653
　　　　　　网购咨询 8610-82303908
印　　刷： 北京富资园科技发展有限公司

版　　次： 2023 年 10 月第 1 版　　**印　　次：** 2024 年 1 月第 2 次印刷
开　　本： 889 毫米 × 1194 毫米 1/16　　**印　　张：** 9.75
字　　数： 191 千字
定　　价： 98.00 元

PRINTED IN CHINA
凡有印装质量问题，本社负责调换。售后 QQ 号 1367565611，电话 010-82303590

编写说明

新丝路"中文+职业技能"系列教材是把中文作为第二语言,结合专业和职业的专门用途、职业用途的中文教材,不是专业理论教材,不是一般意义的通用综合中文教材。本系列教材定位为职场生存中文教材、立体式技能型语言教材。教材研发的目标是既要满足学习者一般中文环境下的基本交际需求,又要满足学习者职业学习需求和职场工作需求。它和普通的国际中文教材的区别不在语法,而在词汇的专门化程度,在中文的用途、使用场合、应用范围。目前,专门用途、职业用途的中文教材在语言分类和研究成果上几近空白,本系列教材的成功研发开创了中文学习的新视野、新领域、新方向,将"中文+职业技能+X等级证书"真正融合,使学习者在学习中文的同时,也可通过实践掌握职业技能,从而获得 X 等级证书。

适用对象

本系列教材将适用对象定位为双零基础(零语言基础、零技能基础)的来华学习中文和先进技能的长期或者短期进修生,可满足初、中、高各层次专业课程的教学需要。教材亦可供海内外相关的培训课程及"走出去"的中资企业培训本土化员工使用。

结构规模

本系列教材采取专项语言技能与职业技能训练相结合的中文教学及教材编写模式。教材选择当前热门的物流管理、汽车服务工程技术、电子商务、机电一体化、计算机网络技术、酒店管理等六个专业,培养各专业急需急用的技术岗位人才。每个专业教材均包括初、中、高级三册。每一册都配有专业视频教学资源,还附有"视频脚本""参考答案"等配套资源。

编写理念

本系列教材将词语进行分类,区分普通词语和专业词语,以通用语料为基础,以概念性、行为性词语为主,不脱离职场情境讨论分级,做到控制词汇量,控制工作场景,控制交流内容与方式,构建语义框架。将语言的分级和专业的分级科学地融合,是实现本系列教材成功编写的关键。

教材目标

语言技能目标:

初级阶段,能熟练掌握基础通用词语和职场的常用专业词语,能使用简短句子进行简单的生活及工作交流。中级阶段，能听懂工作场合简单的交谈与发言，明白大意，把握基本情况，能就工作中重要的话题用简单的话与人沟通。高级阶段，能听懂工作场合一般的交谈与发言，抓住主要内容和关键信息，使用基本交际策略与人交流、开展工作，能初步了解与交际活动相关的文化因素，掌握与交际有关的一般文化背景知识，能排除交际时遇到的文化障碍。交际能力层次的递进实现从初级的常规礼节、基本生活及工作的交流能力，到中级的简单的服务流程信息交流能力，最后达到高级的复杂信息的交流和特情处理的能力。

职业技能目标：

以满足岗位需求为目标，将遴选出的当前热门的专业工作岗位分为初、中、高三级。物流管理专业初、中、高级对应的岗位分别是物流员、物流经理、物流总监；汽车服务工程技术专业初、中、高级对应的岗位分别是汽车机电维修工、汽车服务顾问、技术总监；电子商务专业初、中、高级对应的岗位分别是电子商务运营助理、电子商务运营员、电子商务客服；机电一体化专业初、中、高级对应的岗位分别是机电操作工、机电调整工、机电维修工；计算机网络技术专业初、中、高级对应的岗位分别是宽带运维工程师、网络运维专员、网络管理员；酒店管理专业初、中、高级对应的岗位分别是前厅基层接待员、前厅主管、前厅经理。每个专业分解出三十个工作场景/任务，学习者在学习后能够全面掌握此岗位的概况及基本程序，实现语言学习和专业操作的双重目标。

编写原则

1. 语言知识技能与专业知识技能并进，满足当前热门的、急需急用的岗位需求。
2. 渐进分化，综合贯通，拆解难点，分而治之。
3. 语言知识与专业知识科学、高效复现，语言技能与专业技能螺旋式上升，职场情境、语义框架、本体输入方式相互配合。
4. 使用大量的图片和视频，实现专业知识和技能呈现形式可视化。
5. 强化专业岗位实操性技能。本系列教材配有专业技术教学的视频，突出展示专业岗位的实操性技能，语言学习难度与技能掌握难度的不匹配可通过实操性强的视频和实训环节来补充。

特色追求

本系列教材从初级最基础的语音知识学习和岗位认知开始，将"中文＋职业技能"融入在工作场景对话中，把工作分解成一个个任务，用图片认知的方式解决专业词语的认知问题，用视频展示的方法解决学习者掌握中文词语与专业技能的不匹配问题，注重技能的实操性，注重"在做中学"。每一单元都设置了"学以致用"板块，目的不仅仅是解决本单元任务的词语认知问题，更是将学习的目标放在"能听""能用""能模仿说出"上。我们力争通过大量图片的使用和配套视频的展示，将教材打造成立体式、技能型语言教材，方便学习者能够更好地自主学习。

使用建议

1. 本系列教材每个专业分为初、中、高级三册，每册10单元，初级每单元建议8～10课时完成，中级10～12课时完成，高级12～14课时完成。

2. 教材注释和说明着力于简明扼要，注重实操性，注重听说技能培养，对于教材涉及的语法知识，教师可视情况予以细化和补充。

3. "单元实训"板块可以在课文和语言点学完之后作为课堂练习使用，建议2课时完成。教师要带着学习者按照实训步骤一步步完成，实训步骤不要求学习者能够看懂、读懂，重要的是教师要引领操作，实现学习者掌握专业技能的目标。

4. "单元小结"板块是对整个单元关键词语和核心内容的总结，对于这部分内容，教师要进行听说练习，以便更好地帮助学习者了解本单元的核心工作任务。

5. 教师上课时要充分利用教材设计的练习，引导学习者多听多练，听说结合，学做合一。

6. 教师要带着学习者熟练诵读课文，要求学习者把每课的关键词语和句子、课堂用语背诵下来。

特别感谢

感谢教育部中外语言交流合作中心将新丝路"中文＋职业技能"系列教材列为重点研发项目，为我们教材编写增添了动力和责任感。教材编写委员会负责整套教材的规划、设计与编写协调，并先后召开上百次讨论会，对每册教材的课文编写、体例安排、注释说明、练习设计、图片选择、视频制作等进行全方位的评估、讨论和审定。感谢编写委员会成员和所有编者高度的敬业精神、精益求精的编写态度，以及所投入的热情和精力、付出的心血与智慧。感谢关注本系列教材并贡献宝贵意见的国际中文教育教学界专家和全国各地的同人。

新丝路"中文＋职业技能"系列教材编写委员会

2023年4月

Compilation Instructions

The New Silk Road "Chinese + Vocational Skills" is a series of Chinese textbooks for specialized and vocational purposes that combine professional and vocational technologies with Chinese as a second language. Instead of being specialized theoretical textbooks, or comprehensive or universal Chinese textbooks in a general sense, this series is intended to be Chinese textbooks for career survival, and three-dimensional skills-based language textbooks. The textbooks are developed with a view to meeting students' basic communication needs in general Chinese environment, and their professional learning needs and workplace demands as well. They are different from ordinary Chinese textbooks for foreigners in the degree of specialization of vocabulary, in the purpose, usage occasion, and application scope of Chinese (not in grammar). At present, Chinese textbooks for specialized and vocational purposes are virtually non-existent in terms of language classification and research results, so the successful development of this series has opened up new horizons, new fields and new directions for Chinese learning, and virtually integrated "Chinese + Vocational Skills + X-Level Certificates", which enables students to practically master vocational skills and obtain X-level certificates while learning Chinese.

Applicable Targets

This series is targeted at long-term or short-term students who come to China to learn Chinese and advanced skills with zero language basis and zero skill basis, which can meet the teaching needs of the elementary, intermediate and advanced specialized courses. This series can also be used for relevant training courses at home and abroad and for Chinese-funded enterprises that "go global" to train local employees.

Structure and Scale

This series adopts a Chinese teaching and textbook compilation model combining special language skills and vocational skills training. The series includes the textbooks for six popular majors such as logistics management, automotive service engineering technology, e-commerce, mechatronics, computer networking technology, and hotel management to cultivate technical talents in urgent need. The textbooks for each major consist of the textbooks at the elementary, intermediate and advanced levels. Each textbook is equipped with professional video teaching resources, and "video scripts", "reference answers" and other supporting resources as well.

Compilation Concept

This series classifies the vocabulary into general vocabulary and specialized vocabulary. Based on the general vocabulary, it focuses on conceptual and behavioral words, not deviating from workplace situations, so as to control the vocabulary, work scenarios and content and means of communication, and build the semantic framework. The scientific integration of language classification and specialty classification is the key to the successful compilation of textbooks.

Textbook Objectives

Language Skill Objectives

For students at the elementary level, they are trained to be familiar with basic general vocabulary and common specialized vocabulary in the workplace, and be able to use short sentences for simple communication in life and at work. For those at the intermediate level, they are trained to understand simple conversations and speeches in the workplace, comprehend the main ideas, grasp the basic situations, and communicate with others in simple words on important topics at work. For those at the advanced level, they are trained to be able to understand general conversations and speeches in the workplace, grasp the main content and key information, use basic communication strategies to communicate with others and carry out the work, have a preliminary understanding of cultural factors related to communication activities, master the general communication-related cultural background knowledge, and overcome cultural barriers encountered during communication. The progression in level of communicative competence helps them to leap forward from routine etiquette, basic communication in life and at work at the elementary level, to simple information exchange of service processes at the intermediate level, and finally to complex information exchange and handling of special circumstances at the advanced level.

Vocational Skill Objectives

To meet job requirements at the elementary, intermediate and advanced levels, the professional positions that are most urgently needed overseas are selected. The positions corresponding to logistics management at the elementary, intermediate and advanced levels are logistics staff, logistics managers and logistics directors; the positions corresponding to automotive service engineering technology at the elementary, intermediate and advanced levels are automotive electromechanical maintenance staff, automotive service consultants and technical directors; the positions corresponding to e-commerce at the elementary, intermediate and advanced levels are electronic operation assistants, e-commerce operators and e-commerce customer service staff; the positions corresponding to mechatronics at the elementary, intermediate and advanced levels are mechanical and electrical operators, mechanical and electrical adjusters, and mechanical and electrical maintenance staff; the positions corresponding to computer networking techology at the elementary, intermediate and advanced levels are broadband operation and maintenance engineers, network operation and maintenance specialists, and network administrators; the positions corresponding to hotel management at the elementary, intermediate and advanced levels are lobby receptionists, lobby supervisors and lobby managers. Through 30 work scenarios/tasks set for each major, learners can fully grasp the general situations and basic procedures of the position after learning, and achieve the dual goals of language learning and professional operation.

Principles of Compilation

1. Language knowledge skills and professional knowledge skills go hand in hand to meet the demands of current popular and urgently needed job positions;

2. It makes progressive differentiation and comprehensive integration, breaking down, dividing and conquering difficult points;

3. Language knowledge and professional knowledge recur scientifically and efficiently, language skills and professional skills spiral upward, and the situational stage, semantic framework, and ontology input methods cooperate with each other;

4. Professional knowledge and skills are visualized, using a lot of pictures and videos;

5. It strengthens the practical skills in professional positions. This series of textbooks is equipped with videos of professional technical training, highlighting the practical skills for professional positions. It addresses the mismatch between the difficulty of language learning and that of mastering skills by supplementing with practical videos and practical training.

Characteristic Pursuit

Starting from the basic phonetic knowledge learning and job cognition at the elementary level, this series integrates "Chinese + Vocational Skills" into the working scene dialogues, breaking down the job into various tasks, solving lexical students' problems by means of picture cognition, solving the problem of the mismatch between students' mastery of Chinese vocabulary and professional skills by means of displaying videos, stressing the practicality of skills, and focusing on "learning by doing". Each unit has a "Practicing What You Have Learnt" module, which not only solves the problem of lexical cognition of this unit, but also takes "being able to comprehend", "being able to use" and "being able to imitate" as the learning objectives. We strive to use a large number of pictures and display supporting videos to build the textbooks into three-dimensional skills-based language teaching materials, so that learners can learn more independently.

Recommendations for Use

1. Each major of this series consists of three volumes at the elementary, intermediate, and advanced levels, with 10 units in each volume. For each unit, it is recommended to be completed in 8-10 class hours at the elementary level, 10-12 class hours at the intermediate level, and 12-14 class hours at the advanced level.

2. The notes and explanations in the textbooks focus on conciseness, practicality, and the training of listening and speaking skills. The grammar knowledge in the textbooks can be detailed and supplemented by teachers as the case may be.

3. "Unit Practical Training" module can be used as a classroom exercise after the texts and language points, preferably to be completed in two class hours. Teachers should guide students to complete the training tasks step by step. Students are not required to read and understand the training steps. It is important that teachers guide students to achieve the goal of mastering professional skills.

4. "Unit Summary" module summarizes the keywords and core content of the entire unit. Through listening and speaking exercises, this part can better help learners understand the core tasks of this unit.

5. Teachers should make full use of the exercises designed in the textbooks during class, and guide students to listen more and practice more, combine listening and speaking, and integrate learning with practice.

6. Teachers should guide students to proficiently read the texts aloud, asking them to recite the keywords, sentences and classroom expressions in each unit.

Acknowledgements

We are grateful to the Center for Language Education and Cooperation of the Ministry of Education for listing the New Silk Road "Chinese + Vocational Skills" series as a key research and development project, which adds motivation and a sense of responsibility to our textbook compilation. The Textbook Compilation Committee is responsible for the planning, design, compilation and coordination of the entire set of textbooks, and has held hundreds of seminars to conduct a comprehensive evaluation, discussion, examination and approval of text compilation, style arrangement, notes and explanations, exercise design, picture selection, and video production of each textbook. We are indebted to the members of the Compilation Committee and all compilers for their professional dedication, unwavering pursuit of perfection in the compilation, as well as their enthusiasm, hard work and wisdom. We are thankful to the experts in international Chinese language education and colleagues from all over the country who have kept a close eye on this series and contributed their valuable opinions.

Compilation Committee of New Silk Road "Chinese + Vocational Skills" Series
April 2023

gǎngwèi jièshào
岗位介绍
Jobs Introduction

tiáozhěnggōng
调整工
tool setter

cāozuògōng
操作工
operator

jīxiè wéixiūgōng
机械维修工
mechanic maintenance worker

diànqì wéixiūgōng
电气 维修工
electrical maintenance worker

chēgōng
车工
lathe operator

xǐgōng
铣工
miller

语法术语及缩略形式参照表
Abbreviations of Grammar Terms

Grammar Terms in Chinese	Grammar Terms in Pinyin	Grammar Terms in English	Abbreviations
名词	míngcí	noun	n.
专有名词	zhuānyǒu míngcí	proper noun	pn.
代词	dàicí	pronoun	pron.
数词	shùcí	numeral	num.
量词	liàngcí	measure word	m.
数量词	shùliàngcí	quantifier	q.
动词	dòngcí	verb	v.
助动词	zhùdòngcí	auxiliary	aux.
形容词	xíngróngcí	adjective	adj.
副词	fùcí	adverb	adv.
介词	jiècí	preposition	prep.
连词	liáncí	conjunction	conj.
助词	zhùcí	particle	part.
拟声词	nǐshēngcí	onomatopoeia	onom.
叹词	tàncí	interjection	int.
前缀	qiánzhuì	prefix	pref.
后缀	hòuzhuì	suffix	suf.
成语	chéngyǔ	idiom	idm.
短语	duǎnyǔ	phrase	phr.
主语	zhǔyǔ	subject	S
谓语	wèiyǔ	predicate	P
宾语	bīnyǔ	object	O
定语	dìngyǔ	attributive	Attrib
状语	zhuàngyǔ	adverbial	Adverb
补语	bǔyǔ	complement	C

CONTENTS 目 录

第一单元　机电一体化概述　Unit 1　An Overview of Mechatronics　1

第一部分 语音　Phonetic Learning　2
一、语音知识　Knowledge about Phonetics　2
　1. 声母和韵母（1）Initials and finals (1)　2
　　声母表 Table of initials
　　韵母表 Table of finals
　2. 声调图 Figure of tones　3
二、语音练习　Pronunciation Drills　3

第二部分 课文　Texts　4
一、热身　Warm-up　4
二、课文　Texts　5
三、视听说　Viewing, Listening and Speaking　8
四、学以致用　Practicing What You Have Learnt　9

第三部分 课堂用语　Classroom Expressions　10
第四部分 单元实训　Unit Practical Training　10
机电一体化设备和产品识别比赛
Contest on the Identification of Mechatronics Equipment and Products　10

第五部分 单元小结　Unit Summary　11

第二单元　机电专业岗位　Unit 2　Positions in Electromechanics　15

第一部分 语音　Phonetic Learning　16
一、语音知识　Knowledge about Phonetics　16
　1. 音节 Syllables　16
　2. 声母和韵母（2）Initials and finals (2)　17
　　声母 Initials: b p m f d t n l g k h
　　开口呼韵母 Open-mouth finals
　3. 声调 Tones　17
二、语音练习　Pronunciation Drills　17

I

第二部分　课文　**Texts**		18
一、热身　Warm-up		18
二、课文　Texts		19
三、视听说　Viewing, Listening and Speaking		21
四、学以致用　Practicing What You Have Learnt		22
第三部分　课堂用语　**Classroom Expressions**		23
第四部分　单元实训　**Unit Practical Training**		24
岗位知识汇报和比赛　Report and Contest on the Knowledge of the Jobs		24
第五部分　单元小结　**Unit Summary**		25

第三单元　车间安全培训　Unit 3　Workshop Safety Training　27

第一部分　语音　**Phonetic Learning**		28
一、语音知识　Knowledge about Phonetics		28
1. 声母和韵母（3）Initials and finals (3)		28
声母 Initials: zh ch sh r z c s		
合口呼韵母 Closed-mouth finals		
2. 轻声 Neutral tone		29
二、语音练习　Pronunciation Drills		29
第二部分　课文　**Texts**		29
一、热身　Warm-up		29
二、课文　Texts		31
三、视听说　Viewing, Listening and Speaking		33
四、学以致用　Practicing What You Have Learnt		34
第三部分　课堂用语　**Classroom Expressions**		35
第四部分　单元实训　**Unit Practical Training**		35
车间安全防护用品的使用　Use of Safety Protection Articles in a Workshop		35
第五部分　Part 5　单元小结　**Unit Summary**		36

第四单元　安全标志　Unit 4　Safety Signs　39

第一部分　语音　**Phonetic Learning**		40
一、语音知识　Knowledge about Phonetics		40
声母和韵母（4）Initials and finals (4)		40
声母 Initials: j q x		
齐齿呼、撮口呼韵母 Even-teeth finals and round-mouth finals		
二、语音练习　Pronunciation Drills		41

第二部分 课文 **Texts**	41
一、热身　Warm-up	41
二、课文　Texts	42
三、视听说　Viewing, Listening and Speaking	45
四、学以致用　Practicing What You Have Learnt	45
第三部分 课堂用语 **Classroom Expressions**	46
第四部分 单元实训 **Unit Practical Training**	47
了解安全标志　Understanding Safety Signs	47
第五部分 单元小结 **Unit Summary**	47

第五单元　6S 管理　Unit 5　6S Management　51

第一部分 语音 **Phonetic Learning**	52
一、语音知识　Knowledge about Phonetics	52
1. 拼写规则（1）Spelling rules (1)	52
2. 三声变调 Third-tone sandhi	52
3. "不"的变调 Tone sandhi of "不"	52
二、语音练习　Pronunciation Drills	53
第二部分 课文 **Texts**	53
一、热身　Warm-up	53
二、课文　Texts	54
三、视听说　Viewing, Listening and Speaking	57
四、学以致用　Practicing What You Have Learnt	58
第三部分 课堂用语 **Classroom Expressions**	59
第四部分 单元实训 **Unit Practical Training**	59
现场 6S 管理　On-Site 6S Management	59
第五部分 单元小结 **Unit Summary**	60

第六单元　钳工工具　Unit 6　Fitter's Tools　63

第一部分 语音 **Phonetic Learning**	64
一、语音知识　Knowledge about Phonetics	64
拼写规则（2）Spelling rules (2)	64
二、语音练习　Pronunciation Drills	65

第二部分 课文 Texts	65
一、热身 Warm-up	65
二、课文 Texts	66
三、视听说 Viewing, Listening and Speaking	68
四、学以致用 Practicing What You Have Learnt	69
第三部分 课堂用语 Classroom Expressions	70
第四部分 单元实训 Unit Practical Training	70
了解钳工工具及其使用方法 Understanding Fitter's Tools and Their Uses	70
第五部分 单元小结 Unit Summary	71

第七单元 锉削 Unit 7 Filing — 73

第一部分 语音 Phonetic Learning	74
一、语音知识 Knowledge about Phonetics	74
1. 拼写规则（3）Spelling rules (3)	74
2. "一"的变调 Tone sandhi of "一"	74
二、语音练习 Pronunciation Drills	74
第二部分 课文 Texts	75
一、热身 Warm-up	75
二、课文 Texts	76
三、视听说 Viewing, Listening and Speaking	78
四、学以致用 Practicing What You Have Learnt	79
第三部分 课堂用语 Classroom Expressions	80
第四部分 单元实训 Unit Practical Training	80
了解锉削工具及其使用方法 Understanding Filing Tools and Their Uses	80
第五部分 单元小结 Unit Summary	81

第八单元 划线与锯削 Unit 8 Scribing and Sawing — 83

第一部分 语音 Phonetic Learning	84
一、语音知识 Knowledge about Phonetics	84
1. 拼写规则（4）Spelling rules (4)	84
2. 儿化 Erhua	84
二、语音练习 Pronunciation Drills	85

第二部分 课文 **Texts**	85
一、热身 Warm-up	85
二、课文 Texts	86
三、视听说 Viewing, Listening and Speaking	88
四、学以致用 Practicing What You Have Learnt	89
第三部分 课堂用语 **Classroom Expressions**	90
第四部分 单元实训 **Unit Practical Training**	90
了解划线与锯削的工具及其使用方法 Understanding Scribing and Sawing Tools and Their Uses	90
第五部分 单元小结 **Unit Summary**	91

第九单元 图纸 Unit 9 Drawings — 93

第一部分 语音 **Phonetic Learning**	94
一、语音知识 Knowledge about Phonetics	94
拼写规则（5）：隔音符号的用法 Spelling rules (5): the usage of the syllable-dividing mark	94
二、语音练习 Pronunciation Drills	94
第二部分 课文 **Texts**	95
一、热身 Warm-up	95
二、课文 Texts	97
三、视听说 Viewing, Listening and Speaking	100
四、学以致用 Practicing What You Have Learnt	101
第三部分 课堂用语 **Classroom Expressions**	102
第四部分 单元实训 **Unit Practical Training**	102
认识不同的图纸 Understanding Different Drawings	102
第五部分 单元小结 **Unit Summary**	103

第十单元 测量工具 Unit 10 Measuring Tools — 105

第一部分 语音 **Phonetic Learning**	106
一、语音知识 Knowledge about Phonetics	106
声调的标写 Marking of tones	106
二、语音练习 Pronunciation Drills	106

V

第二部分 课文　Texts　107
- 一、热身　Warm-up　107
- 二、课文　Texts　108
- 三、视听说　Viewing, Listening and Speaking　111
- 四、学以致用　Practicing What You Have Learnt　112

第三部分 课堂用语　Classroom Expressions　113

第四部分 单元实训　Unit Practical Training　113
- 测量工具的识读　Recognition of Measuring Tools　113

第五部分 单元小结　Unit Summary　114

附录　Appendixes　117

词汇总表　Vocabulary	117
视频脚本　Video Scripts	129
参考答案　Reference Answers	133

1

Jīdiàn yìtǐhuà gàishù
机电一体化概述
An Overview of Mechatronics

jīdiàn yìtǐhuà gōngsī
机电一体化公司

gōngzuò huánjìng
工作 环境
working environment of a mechatronics company

shēngchǎn chējiān
生产 车间
production workshop

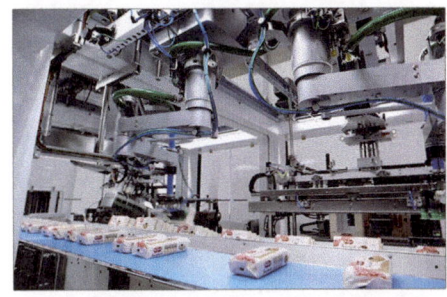

zìdònghuà shēngchǎnxiàn
自动化 生产线
automatic production line

wéixiū chējiān
维修 车间
maintenance workshop

cāngkù
仓库
warehouse

huìyìshì
会议室
conference room

> **题解　Introduction**
>
> 1. 学习内容：机电一体化的构成、机电一体化产品。
>   Learning content: The composition of mechatronics and the mechatronics products
> 2. 知识目标：了解声母、韵母和声调概貌，掌握与机电一体化相关的核心词语及表达。
>   Knowledge objectives: To get a general idea of initials, finals, tones, and grasp the core vocabulary and expressions related to mechatronics
> 3. 技能目标：能识别机电一体化的设备和产品。
>   Skill objective: To be able to identify mechatronics equipment and products

第一部分　Part 1　语音 Phonetic Learning

一、语音知识　yǔyīn zhīshi　Knowledge about Phonetics

1. 声母和韵母（1）Initials and finals (1)

（1）声母表　Table of initials

声母 Initials	国际音标 International Phonetic Alphabet	声母 Initials	国际音标 International Phonetic Alphabet	声母 Initials	国际音标 International Phonetic Alphabet
b	[p]	g	[k]	zh	[tʂ]
p	[pʰ]	k	[kʰ]	ch	[tʂʰ]
m	[m]	h	[x]	sh	[ʂ]
f	[f]	j	[tɕ]	r	[ʐ]
d	[t]	q	[tɕʰ]	z	[ts]
t	[tʰ]	x	[ɕ]	c	[tsʰ]
n	[n]			s	[s]
l	[l]				

（2）韵母表　Table of finals

韵母 Finals	开口呼韵母 Open-mouth Finals	齐齿呼韵母 Even-teeth Finals	合口呼韵母 Closed-mouth Finals	撮口呼韵母 Round-mouth Finals
单韵母 Single Finals	-i[ɿ]、-i[ʅ]	i[i]	u[u]	ü[y]
	a[A]	ia[iA]	ua[uA]	
	o[o]		uo[uo]	
	e[ɤ]			
	er[ər]	ie[iɛ]		üe[yɛ]

机电一体化概述
An Overview of Mechatronics

（续表）

韵母 Finals	开口呼韵母 Open-mouth Finals	齐齿呼韵母 Even-teeth Finals	合口呼韵母 Closed-mouth Finals	撮口呼韵母 Round-mouth Finals
复韵母 Compound Finals	ai[ai]		uai[uai]	
	ei[ei]		uei[uei]	
	ao[au]	iao[iau]		
	ou[ou]	iou[iou]		
鼻韵母 Finals with a Nasal Consonant or Consonants	an[an]	ian[iɛn]	uan[uan]	üan[yan]
	en[ən]	in[in]	uen[uən]	ün[yn]
	ang[aŋ]	iang[iaŋ]	uang[uaŋ]	
	eng[əŋ]	ing[iŋ]	ueng[uəŋ]	
		ong[uŋ]		iong[yŋ]

2. 声调图　Figure of tones

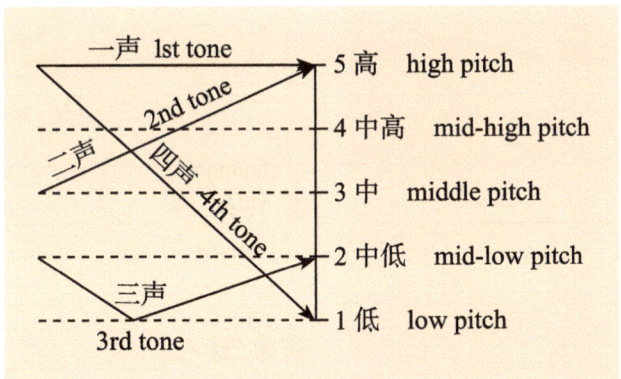

二、语音练习　yǔyīn liànxí　Pronunciation Drills

1. 声韵调拼读　Read aloud and pay attention to the tones.

b + ō = bō　　　　b + ó = bó　　　　b + ǒ = bǒ　　　　b + ò = bò

d + ī = dī　　　　 d + í = dí　　　　 d + ǐ = dǐ　　　　 d + ì = dì

f + ā = fā　　　　 f + á = fá　　　　 f + ǎ = fǎ　　　　 f + à = fà

2. 读一读　Let's read.

① zhǔguǎn 主管　　② xuétú 学徒　　③ jīdiàn yìtǐhuà 机电一体化　　④ jīxiè 机械

⑤ diànqì 电气　　⑥ jìsuànjī jìshù 计算机技术　　⑦ shēngchǎn 生产　　⑧ chējiān 车间

⑨ ānzhuāng 安装　　⑩ shèbèi 设备　　⑪ wéixiū 维修　　⑫ jīqìrén 机器人

第二部分 Part 2

课文 Texts

一、热身 rèshēn Warm-up

1. 给词语选择对应的图片。Choose the corresponding picture for each word.

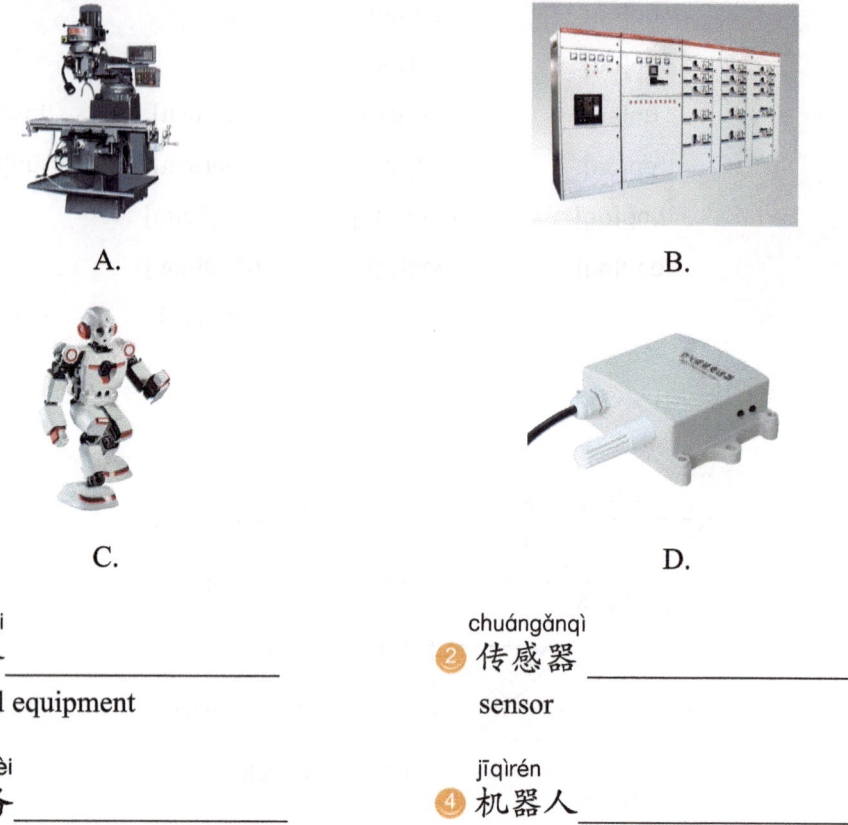

A.

B.

C.

D.

① jīxiè shèbèi
机械设备_____
mechanical equipment

② chuángǎnqì
传感器_____
sensor

③ diànqì shèbèi
电气设备_____
electrical equipment

④ jīqìrén
机器人_____
robot

2. 观看介绍机电一体化公司工作环境的视频，将视频中介绍的地点按先后顺序排列。Watch the video introducing the working environment of mechatronics companies, and arrange the places introduced in the video in sequential order.

liǎojiě jīdiàn yītǐhuà gōngsī gōngzuò huánjìng
了解机电一体化公司工作环境
understand the working environment of mechatronics companies

机电一体化概述
An Overview of Mechatronics

A. shēngchǎn chējiān
   生产 车间
   production workshop

B. huìyìshì
   会议室
   conference room

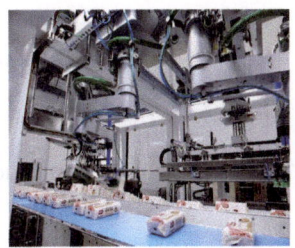

C. zìdònghuà shēngchǎnxiàn
   自动化 生产线
   automatic production line

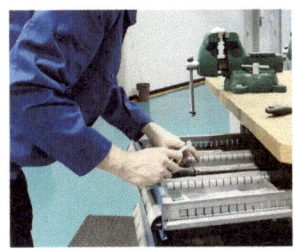

D. wéixiū chējiān
   维修 车间
   maintenance workshop

E. cāngkù
   仓库
   warehouse

二、课文 kèwén Texts

A 01-01

zhǔguǎn: Nǐmen hǎo!
主管：你们好！

xuétú: Nǐ hǎo, zhǔguǎn! Qǐngwèn jīdiàn yìtǐhuà bāokuò nǎxiē nèiróng?
学徒：你好，主管！请问机电一体化包括哪些内容？

zhǔguǎn: Jīdiàn yìtǐhuà yìbān bāokuò jīxiè、diànqì、jìsuànjī jìshù sān gè fāngmiàn.
主管：机电一体化一般包括机械、电气、计算机技术三个方面。

译文 yìwén Text in English

Supervisor: Hello!
Apprentice: Hello, Supervisor! May I ask what mechatronics includes?
Supervisor: It generally includes three fields: mechanical, electrical and computer technology.

普通词语 pǔtōng cíyǔ General Vocabulary 🎧 01-02

1.	你们	nǐmen	pron.	you (*plural*)
2.	好	hǎo	adj.	good, fine
3.	你好	nǐ hǎo	phr.	hello, how do you do
	你	nǐ	pron.	you (*singular*)
4.	请问	qǐngwèn	v.	may I ask
	请	qǐng	v.	please
	问	wèn	v.	ask, inquire
5.	包括	bāokuò	v.	include
6.	哪些	nǎxiē	pron.	which, who, what
7.	内容	nèiróng	n.	content
8.	一般	yìbān	adj.	general, usual
9.	三	sān	num.	three
10.	个	gè	m.	a measure word usually used before a noun having no particular classifier
11.	方面	fāngmiàn	n.	field, aspect, side

专业词语 zhuānyè cíyǔ Specialized Vocabulary 🎧 01-03

1.	主管	zhǔguǎn	n.	supervisor
2.	学徒	xuétú	n.	apprentice
3.	机电一体化	jīdiàn yìtǐhuà	phr.	mechatronics
	机电	jīdiàn	n.	electromechanical equipment
	一体化	yìtǐhuà	v.	integrate
4.	机械	jīxiè	n.	machinery, mechanisms
5.	电气	diànqì	n.	electricity, electric power
6.	计算机技术	jìsuànjī jìshù	phr.	computer technology
	计算机	jìsuànjī	n.	computer
	技术	jìshù	n.	technology, technique

B 🎧 01-04

xuétú: Zhǔguǎn, shēngchǎn chējiān fùzé nǎxiē gōngzuò?
学徒：主管，生产车间负责哪些工作？

zhǔguǎn: Zhǔyào fùzé shēngchǎnxiàn shang de shēngchǎn hé ānzhuāng.
主管：主要负责生产线上的生产和安装。

机电一体化概述 1
An Overview of Mechatronics

xuétú: Wéixiū chējiān fùzé nǎxiē gōngzuò?
学徒：维修车间负责哪些工作？

zhǔguǎn: Zhǔyào fùzé jīxiè、diànqì shèbèi de wéixiū.
主管：主要负责机械、电气设备的维修。

译文 yìwén Text in English

Apprentice: Supervisor, what is the production workshop responsible for?
Supervisor: It is mainly responsible for the production and installation on the production line.
Apprentice: What is the maintenance workshop responsible for?
Supervisor: It is mainly responsible for the maintenance of mechanical and electrical equipment.

普通词语 pǔtōng cíyǔ General Vocabulary 🎧 01-05

1.	负责	fùzé	v.	be responsible for, account for
2.	工作	gōngzuò	n.	work, job
3.	主要	zhǔyào	adj.	main, major
4.	上	shang	n.	used after a noun to indicate the scope of sth.
5.	的	de	part.	used after an attribute when it modifies a noun in the usual way
6.	和	hé	conj.	and

专业词语 zhuānyè cíyǔ Specialized Vocabulary 🎧 01-06

1.	生产	shēngchǎn	v.	produce
2.	车间	chējiān	n.	workshop
3.	生产线	shēngchǎnxiàn	n.	production line
4.	安装	ānzhuāng	v.	install
5.	设备	shèbèi	n.	equipment
6.	维修	wéixiū	v.	maintain

7

三、视听说　shì-tīng-shuō　Viewing, Listening and Speaking

观看介绍机器人构成的视频，将名称和图片上指出的部件相匹配，并模仿说出机器人的主要装置。
Watch the video introducing the composition of a robot, match the names with the parts marked in the picture, and tell the robot's main devices.

A. néngyuán 能源 energy
B. jīxiè zhuāngzhì 机械装置 mechanical device
C. jìsuànjī 计算机 computer
D. chuángǎnqì 传感器 sensor

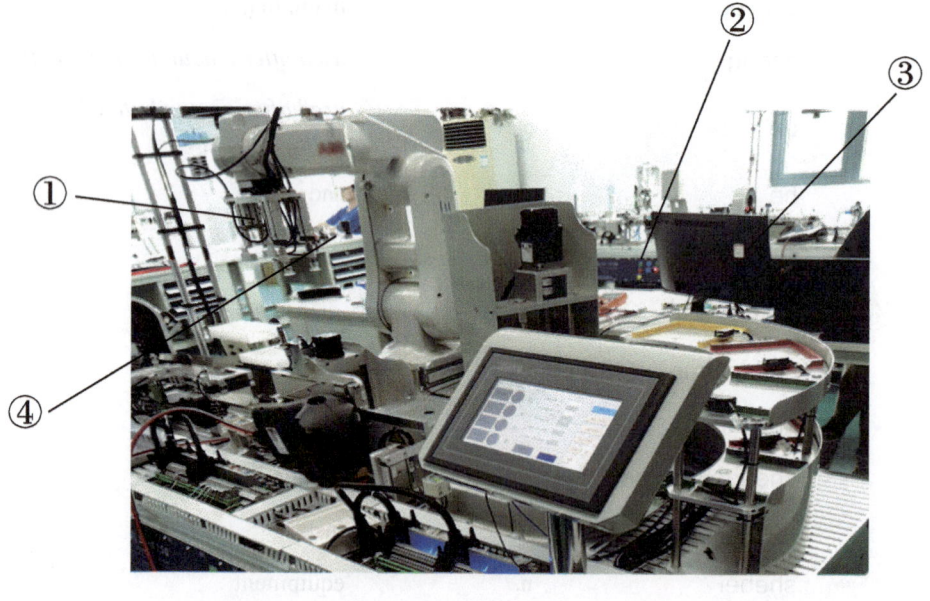

① [　　]　　zhíxíng zhuāngzhì 执行装置 actuator　　② [　　]　　③ [　　]　　④ [　　]

四、学以致用　xuéyǐzhìyòng　Practicing What You Have Learnt

观看介绍机电一体化产品的视频，判断下列物品是否属于机电一体化产品，是的打√，不是的打 ×。Watch the video introducing mechatronics products and tell whether the following items are mechatronics products. Tick (√) for true and cross (×) for false.

bīngxiāng
❶ 冰箱
refrigerator
(　　　)

fùyìnjī
❷ 复印机
copying machine
(　　　)

zhàoxiàngjī
❸ 照相机
camera
(　　　)

bǐjìběn diànnǎo
❹ 笔记本电脑
laptop
(　　　)

qìchē
❺ 汽车
car
(　　　)

zhuō yǐ
❻ 桌椅
desks and a chair
(　　　)

jìngzi
❼ 镜子
mirror
(   )

shǒubiǎo
❽ 手表
(wrist) watch
(   )

第三部分 Part 3 课堂用语 Classroom Expressions

❶ 你好。Nǐ hǎo. Hello.
❷ 现在上课。Xiànzài shàngkè. Class begins now.
❸ 现在下课。Xiànzài xiàkè. Class is over now.

第四部分 Part 4 单元实训 Unit Practical Training

机电一体化设备和产品识别比赛
Contest on the Identification of Mechatronics Equipment and Products

实训目的 Training purpose

通过本次实训，实训人员了解并熟悉机电一体化设备和产品，能够快速说出机电一体化设备和产品的名称，具有团队合作精神、竞争意识。

Through the training, students will understand and get familiar with mechatronics equipment and products, be able to tell mechatronics equipment and products quickly, and develop team spirit and sense of competition.

实训组织 Training organization

每组 5～6 人。

5-6 students in each group

实训步骤 Training steps

❶ 教师带领实训人员参观机电一体化车间，介绍生产线、机械、电气设备和机器人的名称和功能。
The teacher shows the students around the mechatronics workshop, introducing the names and

functions of the production line, mechanical and electrical equipment and robots.

❷ 教师准备好机电一体化设备和产品的图片。将参加实训的人员分成若干小组，每组5～6人。
The teacher prepares pictures of mechatronics equipment and products. Divide the students into groups of 5-6.

❸ 宣布比赛规则及要求：比赛分为必答与抢答两部分，必答题与抢答题各5题，每题10分，共100分。每题需在规定时间15秒内说出答案。每题答对得10分，答错或不答得0分。
Announce the rules and requirements of the competition: The competition is divided into two parts, consisting of five compulsory questions and five rush-answer questions respectively, with ten points for each question and 100 points in total. Each question needs to be answered within 15 seconds. Ten points will be given for each correct answer, and 0 point for a wrong answer or no answer.

任务一：教师出示机电一体化设备的图片，小组成员说出设备名称。
Task 1: The teacher shows pictures of mechatronics equipment, and the group members say the names of the equipment.

任务二：教师出示一些产品的图片，小组成员判断该产品是否为机电一体化产品。
Task 2: The teacher shows pictures of some products, and the group members tell whether they are mechatronics products.

❹ 开始比赛。
Start the competition.

❺ 计算每组得分。
Calculate the score of each group.

❻ 教师总结评价，实训结束。
The teacher summarizes and evaluates, and the training ends.

第五部分 Part 5
单元小结 Unit Summary

词语 cíyǔ Vocabulary

普通词语 General Vocabulary

1.	你们	nǐmen	pron.	you (*plural*)
2.	好	hǎo	adj.	good, fine
3.	你好	nǐ hǎo	phr.	hello, how do you do
	你	nǐ	pron.	you (*singular*)
4.	请问	qǐngwèn	v.	may I ask
	请	qǐng	v.	please
	问	wèn	v.	ask, inquire
5.	包括	bāokuò	v.	include

词语 cíyǔ Vocabulary

6.	哪些	nǎxiē	pron.	which, who, what
7.	内容	nèiróng	n.	content
8.	一般	yìbān	adj.	general, usual
9.	三	sān	num.	three
10.	个	gè	m.	a measure word usually used before a noun having no particular classifier
11.	方面	fāngmiàn	n.	field, aspect, side
12.	负责	fùzé	v.	be responsible for, account for
13.	工作	gōngzuò	n.	work, job
14.	主要	zhǔyào	adj.	main, major
15.	上	shang	n.	used after a noun to indicate the scope of sth.
16.	的	de	part.	used after an attribute when it modifies a noun in the usual way
17.	和	hé	conj.	and

专业词语 Specialized Vocabulary

1.	主管	zhǔguǎn	n.	supervisor
2.	学徒	xuétú	n.	apprentice
3.	机电一体化	jīdiàn yìtǐhuà	phr.	mechatronics
	机电	jīdiàn	n.	electromechanical equipment
	一体化	yìtǐhuà	v.	integrate
4.	机械	jīxiè	n.	machinery, mechanisms
5.	电气	diànqì	n.	electricity, electric power
6.	计算机技术	jìsuànjī jìshù	phr.	computer technology
	计算机	jìsuànjī	n.	computer
	技术	jìshù	n.	technology, technique
7.	生产	shēngchǎn	v.	produce
8.	车间	chējiān	n.	workshop
9.	生产线	shēngchǎnxiàn	n.	production line
10.	安装	ānzhuāng	v.	install
11.	设备	shèbèi	n.	equipment
12.	维修	wéixiū	v.	maintain

机电一体化概述 1
An Overview of Mechatronics

	补充专业词语 Supplementary Specialized Vocabulary			
cíyǔ 词语 Vocabulary	1. 机器人	jīqìrén	n.	robot
	2. 传感器	chuángǎnqì	n.	sensor
	3. 能源	néngyuán	n.	energy
	4. 执行装置	zhíxíng zhuāngzhì	phr.	actuator
	5. 机械装置	jīxiè zhuāngzhì	phr.	mechanical device

jùzi 句子 Sentences

1. 你好。
2. 机电一体化一般包括机械、电气、计算机技术三个方面。
3. 生产车间主要负责生产线上的生产和安装。
4. 维修车间主要负责机械、电气设备的维修。

2. Jīdiàn zhuānyè gǎngwèi
机电专业岗位
Positions in Electromechanics

jīdiàn yìtǐhuà gōngsī gōngzuò gǎngwèi
机电 一体化 公司 工作 岗位
positions in a mechatronics company

zǒngjīnglǐ
总经理
general manager

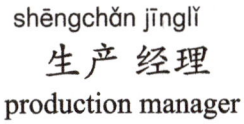

shēngchǎn jīnglǐ
生产 经理
production manager

xiāoshòu jīnglǐ
销售 经理
sales manager

shēngchǎn zhǔguǎn
生产 主管
production supervisor

wéixiū zhǔguǎn
维修 主管
maintenance supervisor

jījiā zhǔguǎn
机加 主管
machining supervisor

> **题解　Introduction**
>
> 1. 学习内容：机电专业岗位名称、机电专业岗位的工作内容。
>   Learning content: The names and job descriptions of positions in electromechanics
> 2. 知识目标：了解音节、声调的基本知识，掌握 b、p、m、f、d、t、n、l、g、k、h 等声母及开口呼韵母的发音，掌握与机电专业岗位相关的核心词语及表达。
>   Knowledge objectives: To have a further study of the basics of syllables and tones, master the pronunciation of initials such as b, p, m, f, d, t, n, l, g, k, h, and acquire the core vocabulary and expressions related to positions in electromechanics
> 3. 技能目标：能辨识各个机电专业岗位。
>   Skill objective: To be able to identify various positions in electromechanics

第一部分　Part 1　语音 Phonetic Learning

一、语音知识　yǔyīn zhīshi　Knowledge about Phonetics

1. 音节　Syllables

汉语的音节一般由声母、韵母和声调组成，音节开头的辅音是声母，声母后面的部分是韵母，韵母上面的部分是声调。例如，在音节"nǐ"中，"n"是声母，"i"是韵母，"ˇ"是声调。音节也可以没有声母，只有韵母和声调，例如"é"。

A Chinese syllable is usually composed of an initial, a final and a tone. The consonant that starts a syllable is called the initial, and the part after the initial is the final. For example, in "nǐ", "n" is the initial, "i" is the final, and "ˇ" is the tone mark. Some syllables do not have initials. A final and a tone can also make a syllable, such as "é".

声母 Initials	韵母 Finals	声调 Tone	音节 Syllable
n	i	ˇ	nǐ
b	a	-	bā
d	ian	ˋ	diàn
h	ao	ˇ	hǎo
	e	ˊ	é

2. 声母和韵母（2） Initials and finals (2)

（1）声母 Initials：b p m f d t n l g k h

声母 Initials	国际音标 International Phonetic Alphabet	声母 Initials	国际音标 International Phonetic Alphabet	声母 Initials	国际音标 International Phonetic Alphabet
b	[p]	d	[t]	g	[k]
p	[pʰ]	t	[tʰ]	k	[kʰ]
m	[m]	n	[n]	h	[x]
f	[f]	l	[l]		

（2）开口呼韵母 Open-mouth finals

开口呼韵母 Open-mouth Finals	国际音标 International Phonetic Alphabet	开口呼韵母 Open-mouth Finals	国际音标 International Phonetic Alphabet	开口呼韵母 Open-mouth Finals	国际音标 International Phonetic Alphabet
-i	[ɿ]	ai	[ai]	an	[an]
-i	[ʅ]	ei	[ei]	en	[ən]
a	[A]	ao	[ɑu]	ang	[ɑŋ]
o	[o]	ou	[ou]	eng	[əŋ]
e	[ɤ]				
er	[ər]				

3. 声调 Tones

汉语是有声调的语言，声调不同，意义就可能不一样。

汉语普通话有四个基本声调。标识声调的符号有四个："‾"表示第一声，"ˊ"表示第二声，"ˇ"表示第三声，"ˋ"表示第四声。调号标在主要元音的上边，例如：mā、má、mǎ、mà。

Chinese is a tonal language. Different tones may result in different meanings.

There are four basic tones in Mandarin Chinese. They are marked as "‾" (the 1st tone), "ˊ" (the 2nd tone), "ˇ" (the 3rd tone) and "ˋ" (the 4th tone) respectively. Tones are marked above the main vowel. For example, "mā", "má", "mǎ", "mà".

二、语音练习 yǔyīn liànxí Pronunciation Drills

读一读 Let's read.

① cāozuògōng 操作工
② tiáozhěnggōng 调整工
③ diàngōng 电工
④ qiángōng 钳工
⑤ tiáozhěng 调整
⑥ shì yùnzhuǎn 试 运转
⑦ jiēxiàn 接线
⑧ chēchuáng 车床
⑨ chēgōng 车工
⑩ xǐchuáng 铣床
⑪ xǐgōng 铣工
⑫ wànyòngbiǎo 万用表

第二部分　Part 2　课文　Texts

一、热身　rèshēn　Warm-up

1. 给词语选择对应的图片。Choose the corresponding picture for each word.

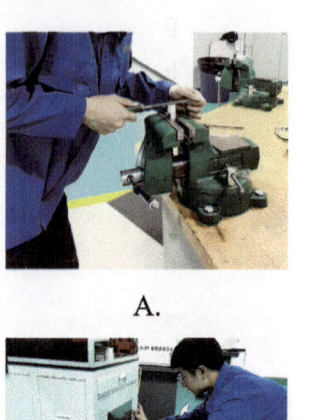

A.

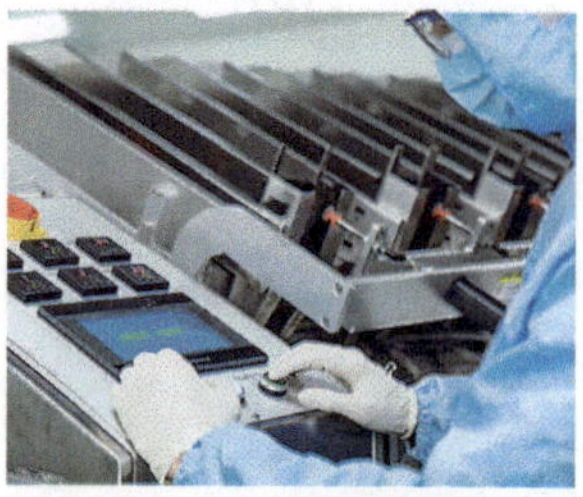

B.

C.

D.

① cāozuògōng
操作工 _____
operator

② diàngōng
电工 _____
electrician

③ qiángōng
钳工 _____
fitter

④ wéixiūgōng
维修工 _____
maintenance worker

2. 观看介绍电工、钳工、维修工的工作内容的视频，选择正确的词语描述他们的工作内容。Watch the video introducing the jobs of electricians, fitters, and maintenance workers, and choose the right words to describe what they do.

diàngōng、qiángōng、wéixiūgōng de gōngzuò nèiróng
电工、钳工、维修工的工作内容
job descriptions of electricians, fitters and maintenance workers

18

机电专业岗位 2
Positions in Electromechanics

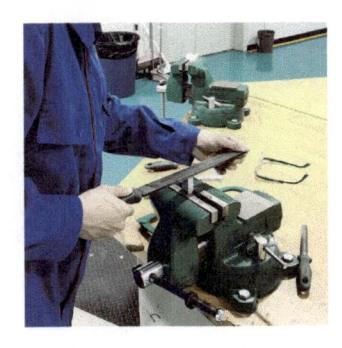

cuòxiāo
A. 锉削
filing

jùxiāo
B. 锯削
sawing

huàxiàn
C. 划线
scribing

jiēxiàn
D. 接线
wiring

wéixiū
E. 维修
maintenance

diàngōng de gōngzuò
① 电工 的 工作 _____
job of an electrician

qiángōng de gōngzuò
② 钳工 的 工作 _____
job of a fitter

wéixiūgōng de gōngzuò
③ 维修工 的 工作 _____
job of a maintenance worker

二、课文 kèwén Texts

A 🎧 02-01

zhǔguǎn: Nǐ hǎo! Wǒ jiào Wáng Wěi, nǐ jiào shénme míngzi?
主管：你好！我 叫 王 伟，你 叫 什么 名字？

xuétú: Nín hǎo, zhǔguǎn! Wǒ jiào Lǐ Míng. Qǐngwèn shēngchǎn chējiān li yǒu nǎxiē gōngzuò
学徒：您好，主管！我 叫 李 明。请问 生产 车间里有哪些 工作

zhǒnglèi?
种类？

19

zhǔguǎn: Shēngchǎn chējiān zhǔyào yǒu cāozuògōng、tiáozhěnggōng、diàngōng hé qiángōng.
主管：生产 车间主要有 操作工、调整工、电工和钳工。

译文 yìwén Text in English

Supervisor: Hello! My name is Wang Wei. What's your name?
Apprentice: Hello, Supervisor! My name is Li Ming. May I ask what kinds of jobs are there in the production workshop?
Supervisor: There are mainly operators, tool setters, electricians and fitters in our workshop.

普通词语 pǔtōng cíyǔ General Vocabulary 02-02

1.	我	wǒ	pron.	I, me
2.	叫	jiào	v.	name, call
3.	王伟	Wáng Wěi	pn.	a person's name
4.	什么	shénme	pron.	used in the interrogative before a noun to ask about people/things
5.	名字	míngzi	n.	name
6.	您	nín	pron.	you (honorific)
7.	李明	Lǐ Míng	pn.	a person's name
8.	里	li	n.	the state of being in/inside
9.	有	yǒu	v.	there is, exist

专业词语 zhuānyè cíyǔ Specialized Vocabulary 02-03

1.	种类	zhǒnglèi	n.	kind, type
2.	操作工	cāozuògōng	n.	operator
3.	调整工	tiáozhěnggōng	n.	tool setter
4.	电工	diàngōng	n.	electrician
5.	钳工	qiángōng	n.	fitter

B 02-04

xuétú: Cāozuògōng yào zuò shénme ne?
学徒：操作工 要做什么呢？

zhǔguǎn: Cāozuògōng yào fùzé shēngchǎn hé ānzhuāng.
主管：操作工 要负责生产和安装。

xuétú: Tiáozhěnggōng ne?
学徒：调整工 呢？

zhǔguǎn: Tiáozhěnggōng zhǔyào fùzé shèbèi de tiáozhěng hé shì yùnzhuǎn.
主管：调整工 主要负责设备的 调整 和试 运转。

译文 yìwén Text in English

Apprentice: What do operators do?
Supervisor: Operators are responsible for production and installation.
Apprentice: What about tool setters?
Supervisor: Tool setters are mainly responsible for the adjustment and test run of the equipment.

普通词语 pǔtōng cíyǔ General Vocabulary 🎧 02-05

1.	要	yào	aux.	should, have to
2.	做	zuò	v.	do
3.	呢	ne	part.	*used at the end of a question*

专业词语 zhuānyè cíyǔ Specialized Vocabulary 🎧 02-06

1.	调整	tiáozhěng	v.	adjust
2.	试运转	shì yùnzhuǎn	phr.	test run
	试	shì	v.	test, try
	运转	yùnzhuǎn	v.	run, operate

三、视听说 shì-tīng-shuō Viewing, Listening and Speaking

观看介绍机电一体化公司工作岗位的视频，将岗位名称放到岗位关系图对应的位置上，并模仿说出主要的岗位名称。Watch the video introducing the positions in a mechatronics company, and put the job titles in the corresponding places of the organizational chart. And then tell the main job titles.

jīdiàn yìtǐhuà gōngsī gōngzuò gǎngwèi
机电一体化 公司 工作 岗位
positions in a mechatronics company

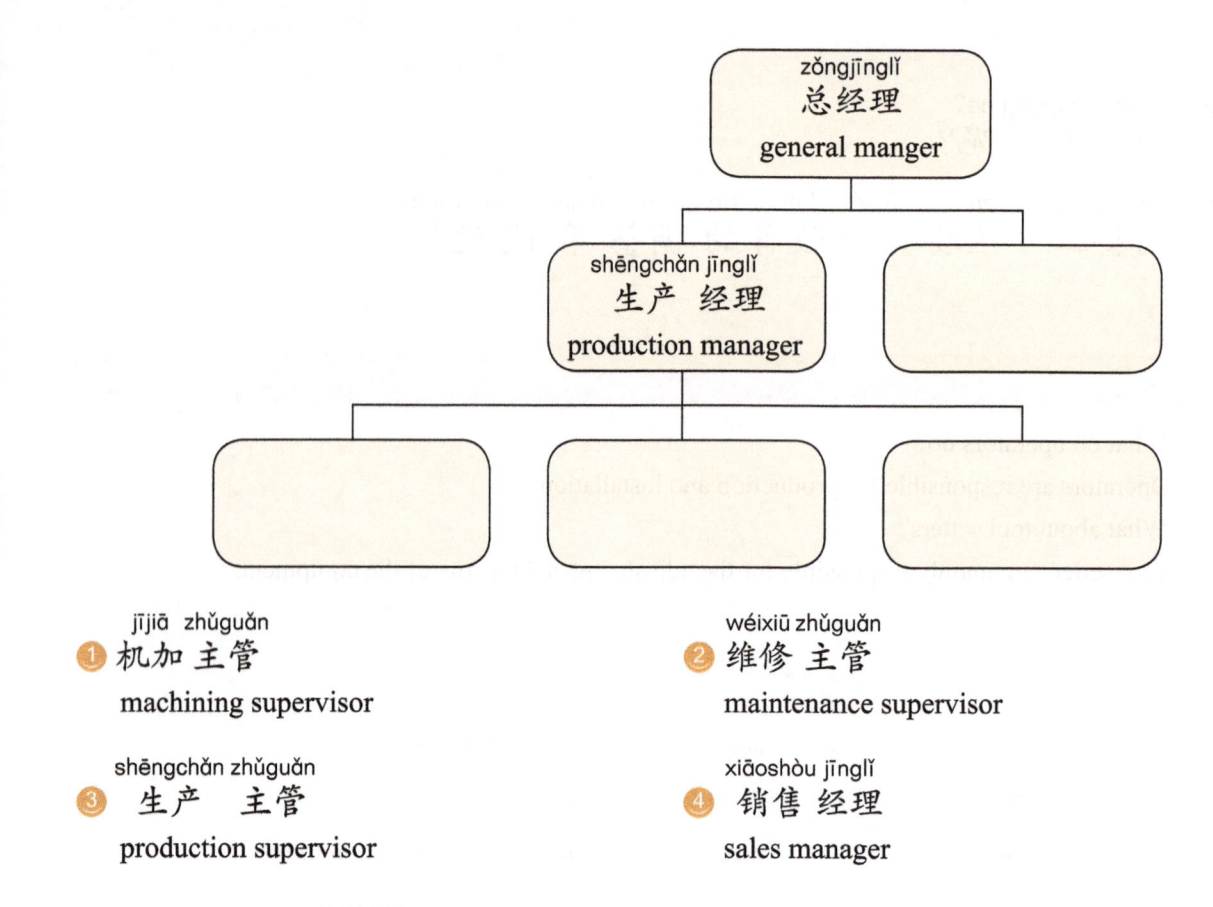

```
                    zǒngjīnglǐ
                    总经理
                   general manger
                        │
            ┌───────────┴───────────┐
        shēngchǎn jīnglǐ
         生 产 经理
       production manager
            │
    ┌───────┼───────┐
   [ ]     [ ]     [ ]
```

① jījiā zhǔguǎn
机加 主管
machining supervisor

② wéixiū zhǔguǎn
维修 主管
maintenance supervisor

③ shēngchǎn zhǔguǎn
生产 主管
production supervisor

④ xiāoshòu jīnglǐ
销售 经理
sales manager

四、学以致用 xuéyǐzhìyòng Practicing What You Have Learnt

观看介绍机电一体化公司工人工作内容的视频，将生产设备或维修工具和岗位名称相匹配。**Watch the video introducing the jobs of workers in a mechatronics company, and match the production equipment or maintenance tools with the job titles.**

chēgōng、xǐgōng、diànqì hé jīxiè wéixiūgōng de gōngzuò nèiróng
车工、铣工、电气和机械维修工的 工作 内容
job descriptions of lathe operators, millers, electrical and mechanical maintenance workers

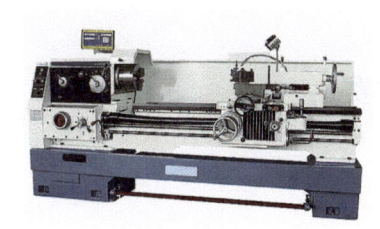

机电专业岗位
Positions in Electromechanics

chēchuáng
A. 车床
lathe

xǐchuáng
B. 铣床
milling machine

wànyòngbiǎo
C. 万用表
multimeter

gōngjùxiāng
D. 工具箱
tool kit

diànqì wéixiūgōng
① 电气 维修工 _____
electrical maintenance worker

chēgōng
② 车工 _____
lathe operator

xǐgōng
③ 铣工 _____
miller

jīxiè wéixiūgōng
④ 机械 维修工 _____
mechanical maintenance worker

第三部分　Part 3
课堂用语　Classroom Expressions

① 跟我读。Gēn wǒ dú. Read after me.
② 读课文。Dú kèwén. Read the text.

23

第四部分　Part 4　单元实训 Unit Practical Training

岗位知识汇报和比赛
Report and Contest on the Knowledge of the Jobs

实训目的 Training purpose

通过本次实训，实训人员了解并熟悉机电一体化常见的工作岗位，能够快速说出岗位名称，具有团队合作精神、竞争意识。

Through the training, the students will understand and get familiar with common jobs in a mechatronics company, be able to tell the job titles quickly, and develop team spirit and sense of competition.

实训组织 Training organization

每组 5～6 人。

5-6 students in each group

实训步骤 Training steps

❶ 将参加实训的人员分成若干小组，每组 5～6 人。采取抽签的方式，每组抽取一个机电一体化岗位。

Divide the students into several groups of 5-6, and each group draws lots and selects a mechatronics position.

❷ 教师将小组成员带到相应的机电一体化工作岗位上，由岗位人员介绍岗位知识和岗位职责，并进行示范。

The teacher takes the group members to the corresponding mechatronics positions, and the position personnel introduce the knowledge and responsibilities of the positions and provide demonstrations.

❸ 参观结束后，每组做一个岗位知识汇报，教师点评。

After the visit, each group makes a presentation of a position, and the teacher makes comments.

❹ 教师准备好机电一体化专业人员在岗位上工作的图片。

The teacher prepares photos of mechatronics professionals working at their posts.

❺ 宣布比赛规则及要求：比赛分为必答与抢答两部分，必答题与抢答题各 5 题，每题 10 分，共 100 分。每题需在规定时间 15 秒内说出图片上专业人员的岗位名称，每题答对得 10 分，答错或不答得 0 分。

Announce the rules and requirements of the contest: The contest is divided into two parts: five compulsory questions and five rush-answer questions. There are ten points for each question and 100 points in total. For each question, the students are required to tell the job titles of the professionals in the pictures within 15 seconds. Ten points will be given for each correct answer, and 0 point for a wrong answer or no answer.

❻ 开始比赛。

Start the contest.

7 计算每组得分。
Calculate the score of each group.

8 教师总结评价，实训结束。
The teacher summarizes and evaluates, and the training ends.

第五部分　Part 5　单元小结 Unit Summary

cíyǔ 词语 Vocabulary

普通词语　General Vocabulary

1.	我	wǒ	pron.	I, me
2.	叫	jiào	v.	name, call
3.	王伟	Wáng Wěi	pn.	a person's name
4.	什么	shénme	pron.	used in the interrogative before a noun to ask about people/things
5.	名字	míngzi	n.	name
6.	您	nín	pron.	you (*honorific*)
7.	李明	Lǐ Míng	pn.	a person's name
8.	里	li	n.	the state of being in/inside
9.	有	yǒu	v.	there is, exist
10.	要	yào	aux.	should, have to
11.	做	zuò	v.	do
12.	呢	ne	part.	used at the end of a question

专业词语　Specialized Vocabulary

1.	种类	zhǒnglèi	n.	kind, type
2.	操作工	cāozuògōng	n.	operator
3.	调整工	tiáozhěnggōng	n.	tool setter
4.	电工	diàngōng	n.	electrician
5.	钳工	qiángōng	n.	fitter
6.	调整	tiáozhěng	v.	adjust
7.	试运转	shì yùnzhuǎn	phr.	test run
	试	shì	v.	test, try
	运转	yùnzhuǎn	v.	run, operate

	补充专业词语		Supplementary Specialized Vocabulary	
cíyǔ **词语** Vocabulary	1. 接线	jiē//xiàn	v.	connect a cable, wire
	2. 车床	chēchuáng	n.	lathe
	3. 车工	chēgōng	n.	lathe operator
	4. 铣床	xǐchuáng	n.	milling machine
	5. 铣工	xǐgōng	n.	miller
	6. 万用表	wànyòngbiǎo	n.	multimeter
	7. 工具箱	gōngjùxiāng	n.	tool kit

jùzi
句子
Sentences

1. 生产车间主要有操作工、调整工、电工和钳工。
2. 操作工要负责生产和安装。
3. 调整工主要负责设备的调整和试运转。

3 车间安全培训
Chējiān ānquán péixùn
Workshop Safety Training

---

jīdiàn shèbèi ānquán cāozuò guīchéng
机电设备 安全 操作 规程
safe operation rules for electromechanical equipment

qīngchú bú bìyào wùjiàn, bǎozhèng láiqù chàngtōng
清除 不 必要 物件，保证 来去 畅通
remove unnecessary objects to keep the passage clear

zhèngquè chuāndài hǎo láobǎo yòngpǐn
正确 穿戴 好劳保 用品
correctly wear labor protection articles

jiǎnchá jīdiàn shèbèi de gègè bùjiàn hé fánghù zhuāngzhì
检查 机电 设备 的 各个 部件 和 防护 装置
check various parts and protective devices of the electromechanical equipment

shèbèi yùnzhuǎn shí, cāozuòzhě bù néng líkāi, yīng xìxīn guānchá
设备 运转 时，操作者 不能 离开，应 细心 观察
when the equipment is running, the operator cannot leave and should observe it carefully

gōngzuò jiéshù qiēduàn diànyuán
工作 结束 切断 电源
cut off the power at the end of the work

qīnglǐ gōngjù hé shèbèi
清理 工具 和 设备
clean up the tools and the equipment

27

> **题解　Introduction**
>
> 1. 学习内容：车间安全防护用品的名称、机电设备安全操作规程。
>   Learning content: The names of workshop safety protection articles, and the safe operation rules for electromechanical equipment
> 2. 知识目标：掌握 zh、ch、sh、r、z、c、s 等声母及合口呼韵母的发音，了解轻声的基本知识，掌握与车间安全培训相关的核心词语及表达。
>   Knowledge objectives: To have a basic understanding of the neutral tone, master the pronunciation of initials such as zh, ch, sh, r, z, c, s and closed-mouth finals, and grasp the core vocabulary and expressions related to workshop safety training
> 3. 技能目标：能正确使用车间安全防护用品。
>   Skill objective: To be able to correctly use safety protection articles in the workshop

第一部分　Part 1　语音 Phonetic Learning

一、语音知识　yǔyīn zhīshi　Knowledge about Phonetics

1. 声母和韵母（3）　Initials and finals (3)

（1）声母 Initials：zh ch sh r z c s

声母 Initials	国际音标 International Phonetic Alphabet	声母 Initials	国际音标 International Phonetic Alphabet
zh	[tʂ]	z	[ts]
ch	[tʂʰ]	c	[tsʰ]
sh	[ʂ]	s	[s]
r	[ʐ]		

（2）合口呼韵母 Closed-mouth finals

合口呼韵母 Closed-mouth Finals	国际音标 International Phonetic Alphabet	合口呼韵母 Closed-mouth Finals	国际音标 International Phonetic Alphabet	合口呼韵母 Closed-mouth Finals	国际音标 International Phonetic Alphabet
u	[u]	uai	[uai]	uang	[uaŋ]
ua	[uA]	uei	[uei]	ueng	[uəŋ]
uo	[uo]	uan	[uan]	ong	[uŋ]
		uen	[uən]		

2. 轻声 Neutral tone

汉语里有些音节不带声调，念得又短又轻，拼写时不标号，这种念得又短又轻的声调叫轻声。例如：爸爸（bàba，dad）、妈妈（māma，mom）。

The neutral tone is pronounced lightly and briefly without any stress, and is indicated in Pinyin by the absence of any tone mark above the syllable. For example, "爸爸"（bàba, dad），"妈妈"（māma, mom）.

二、语音练习 yǔyīn liànxí Pronunciation Drills

读一读 Let's read.

① láobǎo 劳保
② yòngpǐn 用品
③ shàngbān 上班
④ chuāndài 穿戴
⑤ fánghù 防护
⑥ shìgù 事故
⑦ ānquán 安全
⑧ gōngzuòfú 工作服
⑨ ānquánxié 安全鞋
⑩ ānquán yǎnjìng 安全眼镜
⑪ kùfáng 库房
⑫ ānquánmào 安全帽

第二部分 Part 2
课文 Texts

一、热身 rèshēn Warm-up

1. 给词语选择对应的图片。 Choose the corresponding picture for each word.

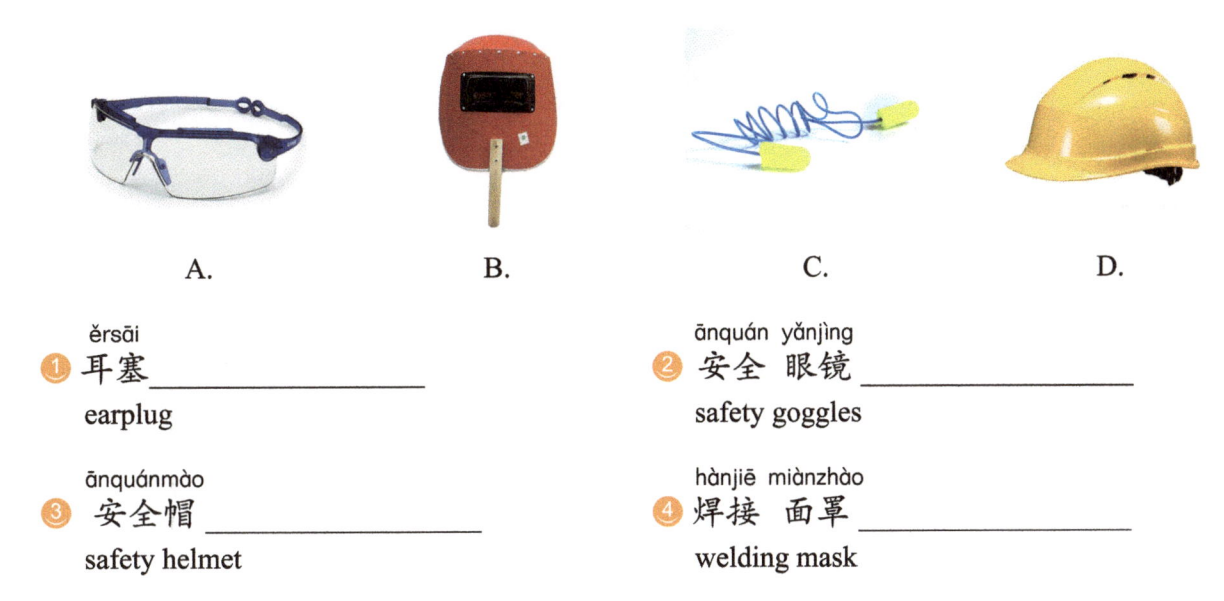

A.   B.   C.   D.

① ěrsāi 耳塞＿＿＿＿＿＿＿
earplug

② ānquán yǎnjìng 安全 眼镜＿＿＿＿＿＿＿
safety goggles

③ ānquánmào 安全帽＿＿＿＿＿＿＿
safety helmet

④ hànjiē miànzhào 焊接 面罩＿＿＿＿＿＿＿
welding mask

2. 观看介绍劳保用品的视频，将图中所示劳保用品和正确词语相匹配。Watch the video introducing labor protection articles and match the labor protection articles shown in the picture with the correct words.

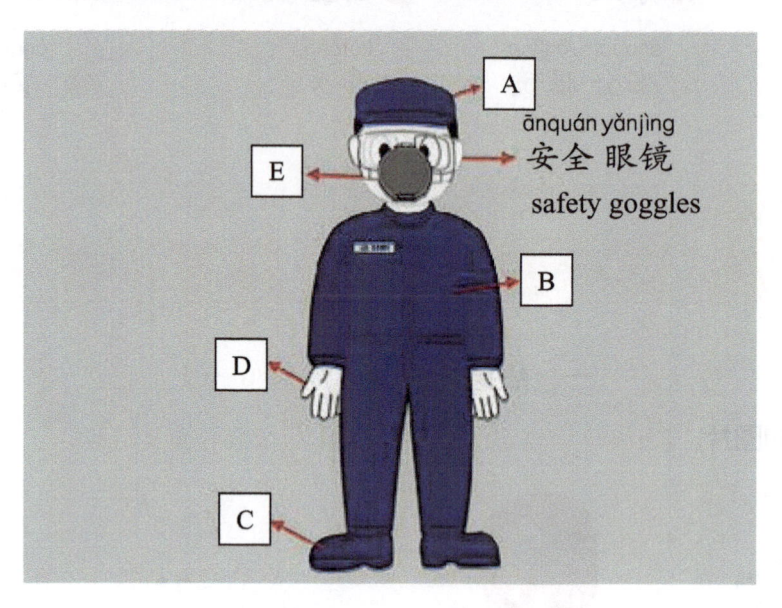

ānquán yǎnjìng
安全 眼镜
safety goggles

① gōngzuòfú
工作服 _____
work clothes

② màozi
帽子 _____
cap

③ shǒutào
手套 _____
gloves

④ ānquánxié
安全鞋 _____
safety shoes

⑤ fángchén kǒuzhào
防尘 口罩 _____
dust mask

二、课文 kèwén Texts

A 03-01

xuétú: Zhǔguǎn, shénme shì láobǎo yòngpǐn?
学徒：主管，什么是劳保用品？

zhǔguǎn: Shì shàngbān shí yào chuāndài de yìxiē gèrén fánghù yòngpǐn.
主管：是上班时要穿戴的一些个人防护用品。

xuétú: Shàngbān shí wèi shénme yào chuāndài tāmen ne?
学徒：上班时为什么要穿戴它们呢？

zhǔguǎn: Zhèyàng kěyǐ yùfáng hé jiǎnshǎo shìgù, bǎozhàng ānquán. Rúguǒ hái yǒu wèntí, jiā wǒ de wēixìn, hàomǎ shì yāo sān líng qī líng líng qī jiǔ wǔ èr líng, yě shì wǒ de shǒujī hào.
主管：这样可以预防和减少事故，保障安全。如果还有问题，加我的微信，号码是 13070079520，也是我的手机号。

译文 yìwén Text in English

Apprentice: Supervisor, what are labor protection articles?
Supervisor: They are some personal protective articles that we need to wear at work.
Apprentice: Why should we wear them at work?
Supervisor: This can prevent and reduce accidents, and ensure safety. If you have any more questions, you can add me on WeChat. The number is 13070079520, which is also my mobile phone number.

普通词语 pǔtōng cíyǔ General Vocabulary 03-02

1.	是	shì	v.	be
2.	时	shí	n.	time
3.	一些	yìxiē	q.	some
4.	为什么	wèi shénme	pron.	why, for what reason
5.	它们	tāmen	pron.	they, them
6.	这样	zhèyàng	pron.	this
7.	可以	kěyǐ	aux.	may, can
8.	如果	rúguǒ	conj.	if
9.	还	hái	adv.	also, as well
10.	问题	wèntí	n.	question, problem
11.	加	jiā	v.	add
12.	微信	wēixìn	n.	WeChat
13.	号码	hàomǎ	n.	number

14.	也	yě	adv.	also, too
15.	手机	shǒujī	n.	mobile phone
16.	号	hào	n.	number

专业词语 zhuānyè cíyǔ Specialized Vocabulary 🎧 03-03

1.	劳保	láobǎo	n.	labor protection
2.	用品	yòngpǐn	n.	articles for use
3.	上班	shàng//bān	v.	work
4.	穿戴	chuāndài	v.	wear
	穿	chuān	v.	put on, wear
	戴	dài	v.	wear (a hat, a mask, etc.)
5.	个人	gèrén	n.	person, individual
6.	防护	fánghù	v.	protect
7.	预防	yùfáng	v.	take precautions against, prevent
8.	减少	jiǎnshǎo	v.	reduce
9.	事故	shìgù	n.	accident
10.	保障	bǎozhàng	v.	protect, ensure
11.	安全	ānquán	adj.	safe

B 🎧 03-04

zhǔguǎn: Jīntiān wǒ jiāo dàjiā rúhé chuāndài láobǎo yòngpǐn.
主管：今天我教大家如何穿戴劳保用品。

xuétú: Hǎo de.
学徒：好的。

zhǔguǎn: Zài shàngbān qījiān, nǐmen yào chuān gōngzuòfú hé ānquánxié, jìnrù chējiān hòu,
主管：在上班期间，你们要穿工作服和安全鞋，进入车间后，

yào àn yāoqiú dài ānquán yǎnjìng. Qù kùfáng shí, yào dài ānquánmào.
要按要求戴安全眼镜。去库房时，要戴安全帽。

译文 yìwén Text in English

Supervisor: Today I will teach you how to wear labor protection articles.
Apprentice: All right.
Supervisor: During working hours, you should wear work clothes and safety shoes. After entering the workshop, wear safety goggles as required. Wear a safety helmet when you go to the warehouse.

车间安全培训 3
Workshop Safety Training

普通词语 pǔtōng cíyǔ General Vocabulary 🎧 03-05

1.	今天	jīntiān	n.	today
2.	教	jiāo	v.	teach
3.	大家	dàjiā	pron.	everybody, everyone
4.	如何	rúhé	pron.	how
5.	好的	hǎo de	phr.	all right
6.	在	zài	prep.	used to indicate time, scope, place, condition, etc.
7.	期间	qījiān	n.	period, course
8.	进入	jìnrù	v.	enter
9.	后	hòu	n.	(of time) (in) future, later time
10.	按	àn	prep.	according to
11.	要求	yāoqiú	n./v.	requirement; require
12.	去	qù	v.	go

专业词语 zhuānyè cíyǔ Specialized Vocabulary 🎧 03-06

1.	工作服	gōngzuòfú	n.	work clothes
2.	安全鞋	ānquánxié	n.	safety shoes
3.	安全眼镜	ānquán yǎnjìng	phr.	safety goggles
	眼镜	yǎnjìng	n.	glasses, spectacles
4.	库房	kùfáng	n.	warehouse
5.	安全帽	ānquánmào	n.	safety helmet

三、视听说 shì-tīng-shuō Viewing, Listening and Speaking

观看介绍安全帽佩戴方法的视频，判断下面安全帽的佩戴方法是否正确，对的打√，错的打×，并模仿说出佩戴安全帽的注意要点。Watch the video introducing the way to wear a safety helmet, and tell whether the following helmets are worn correctly. Tick (√) for true and cross (×) for false. Tell the essentials for wearing a safety helmet.

ānquánmào de pèidài
安全帽 的 佩戴
correct way to wear safety helmets

33

中文 + 机电一体化（初级）

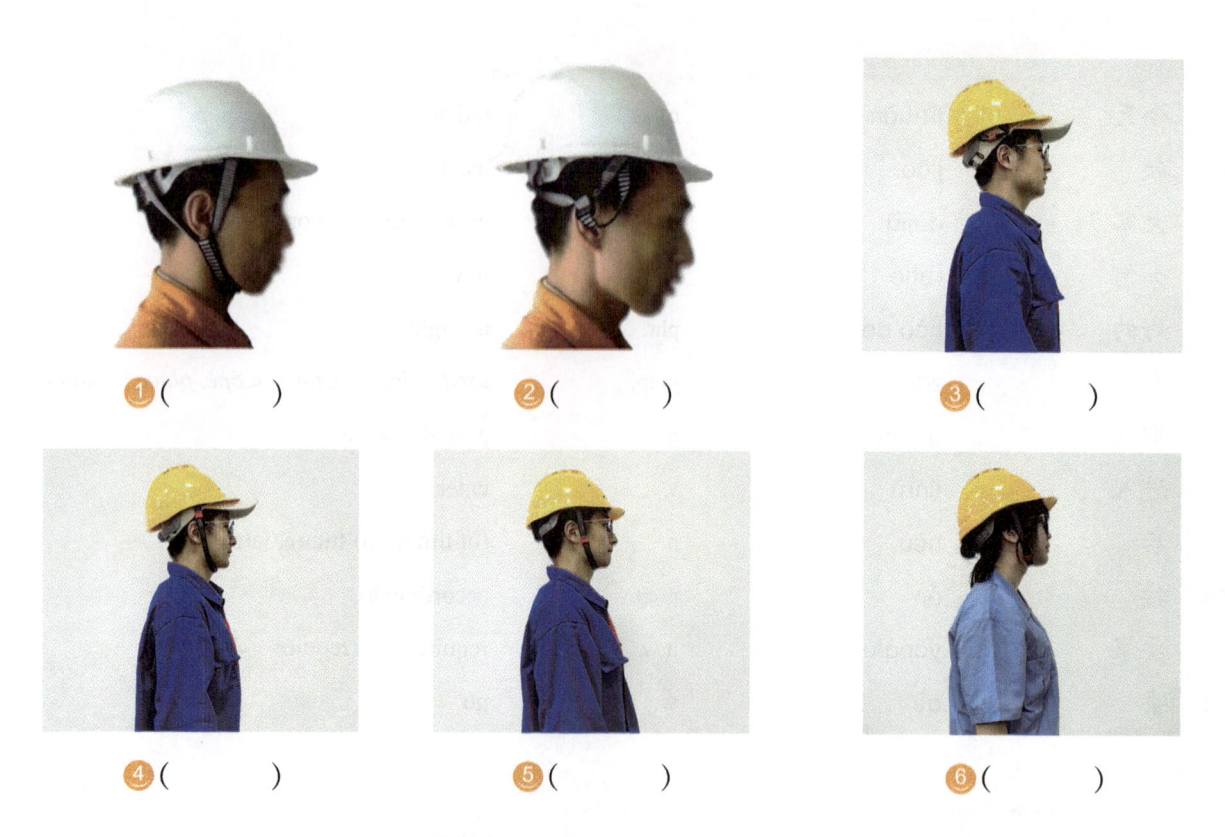

① (　　)　　② (　　)　　③ (　　)

④ (　　)　　⑤ (　　)　　⑥ (　　)

四、学以致用　xuéyǐzhìyòng　Practicing What You Have Learnt

观看介绍机电设备安全操作规程的视频，将下列图片按视频里介绍的步骤排序。**Watch the video introducing safe operation rules for electromechanical equipment, and sequence the following pictures according to the steps described in the video.**

jīdiàn shèbèi ānquán cāozuò guīchéng
机电 设备 安全 操作 规 程
safe operation rules for electromechanical equipment

A.
guānchá shèbèi yùnxíng
观察　设备　运行
observe the running of the equipment

B.
chuāndài láobǎo yòngpǐn
穿戴　劳保　用品
wear labor protection articles

C.
qīnglǐ xiànchǎng
清理　现场
clean up the site

车间安全培训 3
Workshop Safety Training

D.
qiēduàn diànyuán
切断 电源
cut off the power

E.
jiǎnchá shèbèi
检查 设备
check the equipment

F.
qīnglǐ gōngjù
清理 工具
clean up the tools

☐ → ☐ → ☐ → ☐ → ☐ → ☐

第三部分　Part 3　课堂用语 Classroom Expressions

❶ 有问题吗？ Yǒu wèntí ma? Do you have any questions?
❷ 请再说一遍。 Qǐng zài shuō yí biàn. Please say it again.

第四部分　Part 4　单元实训 Unit Practical Training

车间安全防护用品的使用
Use of Safety Protection Articles in a Workshop

实训目的 Training purpose

通过本次实训，实训人员能够认识各种防护用品，学会正确的穿戴方法。

Through the training, the students will be able to know all kinds of safety protection articles and learn the right way to wear them.

实训组织 Training organization

每组5～6人，选举一个组长。组长负责领取本组成员的劳保用品。

Students work in groups of 5-6 and select a leader for each group. The group leader is responsible for getting the group members' labor protection articles.

实训步骤 Training steps

❶ 教师通过视频分享在机电一体化车间里没有正确使用劳保用品造成损害的案例，强调使用劳保用品的必要性。

The teacher uses the video to share the cases of damage caused by incorrect use of labor protection articles in the mechatronics workshops to emphasize the necessity of using labor protection articles.

❷ 教师通过实物展示劳保用品，介绍各类劳保用品的名称和用途，指导实训人员穿戴各类劳保用品。

The teacher shows the labor protection articles in kind, introduces the names and uses of all kinds of labor protection articles, and guides the students to wear all kinds of labor protection articles.

❸ 将实训人员分成若干小组，每组5～6人。采取抽签的方式，每组抽取一个劳保用品。组员介绍该劳保用品的用途和使用场合，并在大家面前正确穿戴。

Divide the students into groups of 5-6. Each group draws lots and get a labor article. The group members introduce its function and use occasions, and then put it on in front of everyone.

❹ 教师对组员介绍的内容进行点评和补充，实训结束。

The teacher comments on and supplements the group members' introduction and the training ends.

第五部分　Part 5　单元小结　Unit Summary

cíyǔ 词语　Vocabulary

普通词语　General Vocabulary

1.	是	shì	v.	be
2.	时	shí	n.	time
3.	一些	yìxiē	q.	some
4.	为什么	wèi shénme	pron.	why, for what reason
5.	它们	tāmen	pron.	they, them
6.	这样	zhèyàng	pron.	this
7.	可以	kěyǐ	aux.	may, can
8.	如果	rúguǒ	conj.	if
9.	还	hái	adv.	also, as well
10.	问题	wèntí	n.	question, problem
11.	加	jiā	v.	add
12.	微信	wēixìn	n.	WeChat
13.	号码	hàomǎ	n.	number
14.	也	yě	adv.	also, too
15.	手机	shǒujī	n.	mobile phone
16.	号	hào	n.	number

车间安全培训
Workshop Safety Training

cíyǔ
词语
Vocabulary

17.	今天	jīntiān	n.	today
18.	教	jiāo	v.	teach
19.	大家	dàjiā	pron.	everybody, everyone
20.	如何	rúhé	pron.	how
21.	好的	hǎo de	phr.	all right
22.	在	zài	prep.	*used to indicate time, scope, place, condition, etc.*
23.	期间	qījiān	n.	period, course
24.	进入	jìnrù	v.	enter
25.	后	hòu	n.	(of time) (in) future, later time
26.	按	àn	prep.	according to
27.	要求	yāoqiú	n./v.	requirement; require
28.	去	qù	v.	go

专业词语　Specialized Vocabulary

1.	劳保	láobǎo	n.	labor protection
2.	用品	yòngpǐn	n.	articles for use
3.	上班	shàng//bān	v.	work
4.	穿戴	chuāndài	v.	wear
	穿	chuān	v.	put on, wear
	戴	dài	v.	wear (a hat, a mask, etc.)
5.	个人	gèrén	n.	person, individual
6.	防护	fánghù	v.	protect
7.	预防	yùfáng	v.	take precautions against, prevent
8.	减少	jiǎnshǎo	v.	reduce
9.	事故	shìgù	n.	accident
10.	保障	bǎozhàng	v.	protect, ensure
11.	安全	ānquán	adj.	safe
12.	工作服	gōngzuòfú	n.	work clothes
13.	安全鞋	ānquánxié	n.	safety shoes
14.	安全眼镜	ānquán yǎnjìng	phr.	safety goggles
	眼镜	yǎnjìng	n.	glasses, spectacles
15.	库房	kùfáng	n.	warehouse
16.	安全帽	ānquánmào	n.	safety helmet

	补充专业词语 Supplementary Specialized Vocabulary			
cíyǔ 词语 Vocabulary	1. 耳塞	ěrsāi	n.	earplug
	2. 焊接面罩	hànjiē miànzhào	phr.	welding mask
	3. 手套	shǒutào	n.	gloves
	4. 防尘口罩	fángchén kǒuzhào	phr.	dust mask

jùzi
句子
Sentences

1. 劳保用品是上班时要穿戴的一些个人防护用品。
2. 穿戴劳保用品可以预防和减少事故，保障安全。
3. 如果还有问题，加我的微信。
4. 在上班期间，你们要穿工作服和安全鞋。
5. 进入车间后，要按要求戴安全眼镜。
6. 去库房时，要戴安全帽。

4

Ānquán biāozhì
安全标志
Safety Signs

ānquán biāozhì de zhǒnglèi
安全 标志 的 种类
types of safety signs

注意安全 Caution	必须戴安全帽	急救点	禁止吸烟 NO SMOKING
jǐnggào biāozhì 警告 标志 warning signs	zhǐshì biāozhì 指示 标志 direction signs	jiùhù biāozhì 救护 标志 first-aid signs	jìnzhǐ biāozhì 禁止 标志 prohibition signs

39

题解　Introduction

1. 学习内容：安全标志的图标、不同安全标志的含义。
   Learning content: The icons of safety signs and the meanings of various safety signs
2. 知识目标：掌握 j、q、x 等声母及齐齿呼、撮口呼韵母的发音，掌握与安全标志相关的核心词语及表达。
   Knowledge objectives: To master the pronunciation of initials, such as j, q, and x, as well as even-teeth finals and round-mouth finals, and acquire the core vocabulary and expressions related to safety signs
3. 技能目标：能辨别安全标志的含义。
   Skill objective: To be able to distinguish the meanings of safety signs

第一部分　Part 1
语音　Phonetic Learning

一、语音知识　yǔyīn zhīshi　Knowledge about Phonetics

声母和韵母（4）Initials and finals (4)

（1）声母 Initials：j q x

声母 Initial	国际音标 International Phonetic Alphabet	声母 Initial	国际音标 International Phonetic Alphabet	声母 Initial	国际音标 International Phonetic Alphabet
j	[tɕ]	q	[tɕʰ]	x	[ɕ]

（2）齐齿呼、撮口呼韵母 Even-teeth finals and round-mouth finals

齐齿呼韵母 Even-teeth finals

齐齿呼韵母 Even-teeth Final	国际音标 International Phonetic Alphabet	齐齿呼韵母 Even-teeth Finals	国际音标 International Phonetic Alphabet	齐齿呼韵母 Even-teeth Finals	国际音标 International Phonetic Alphabet
i	[i]	ia	[iA]	ian	[iɛn]
		ie	[iɛ]	in	[in]
		iao	[iau]	iang	[iɑŋ]
		iou	[iou]	ing	[iŋ]

撮口呼韵母 Round-mouth finals

撮口呼韵母 Round-mouth Final	国际音标 International Phonetic Alphabet	撮口呼韵母 Round-mouth Final	国际音标 International Phonetic Alphabet	撮口呼韵母 Round-mouth Finals	国际音标 International Phonetic Alphabet
ü	[y]	üe	[yɛ]	üan	[yan]
				ün	[yn]
				iong	[yŋ]

二、语音练习　yǔyīn liànxí　Pronunciation Drills

1. 听读辨音　Listen, read and discriminate the sounds.　🎧 04-01

j—zh	q—ch	x—sh
ju—zhu	qu—chu	xu—shu
ji—zhi	qi—chi	xi—shi
jie—zhe	qian—chan	xian—shan
jia—zha	qiao—chao	xie—she
jin—zhen	qin—chen	xing—sheng
jiu—zhou	qing—cheng	xiang—shang

2. 听读辨调　Listen, read and discriminate the tones.　🎧 04-02

yuè—yuē	jiā—jià	qī—qǐ	xué—xuè
yǔ—yú	jiǔ—jiù	qián—qiǎn	xī—xǐ
yīng—yǐng	jīn—jǐn	qù—qǔ	xiè—xiě
yòu—yǒu	jìng—jīng	qǐng—qīng	xíng—xìng
yān—yán	jiāng—jiàng	qiū—qiú	xiǎo—xiào

3. 读一读　Let's read.

① ānquán biāozhì　安全 标志
② ānquán tōngdào　安全 通道
③ tèdìng　特定
④ xìnxī　信息
⑤ zhǐshì biāozhì　指示 标志
⑥ jǐnggào biāozhì　警告 标志
⑦ jìnzhǐ biāozhì　禁止 标志
⑧ jiùhù biāozhì　救护 标志
⑨ gāoyādiàn　高压电
⑩ jìnzhǐ pāizhào　禁止 拍照
⑪ jìnzhǐ xīyān　禁止 吸烟
⑫ dāngxīn chùdiàn　当心 触电

第二部分　Part 2
课文　Texts

一、热身　rèshēn　Warm-up

1. 给词语选择对应的图片。 Choose the corresponding picture for each word.

A. 注意安全 Caution
B. 禁止吸烟 NO SMOKING
C. 必须戴安全帽
D. 急救点

41

中文＋机电一体化（初级）

jíjiùdiǎn
① 急救点 _____
first aid point

zhùyì ānquán
② 注意安全 _____
caution

jìnzhǐ xīyān
③ 禁止吸烟 _____
no smoking

bìxū pèidài ānquánmào
④ 必须佩戴 安全帽 _____
safety helmet must be worn

2. 观看介绍安全标志的视频，为不同的安全标志分类，把对应的字母填写到相应的横线处。
Watch the video introducing safety signs. Classify different safety signs and fill in the corresponding letters.

rènshi ānquán biāozhì
认识 安全 标志
understand safety signs

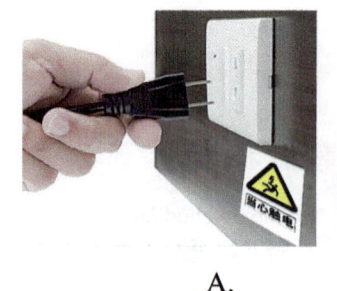

A. 　　　　B. 　　　　C. 　　　　D.

jǐnggào biāozhì
① 警告 标志 _____
warning signs

jìnzhǐ biāozhì
② 禁止 标志 _____
prohibition signs

二、课文　kèwén　Texts

A 🎧 04-03

xuétú: Zhǔguǎn, zhè shì shénme yánsè?
学徒：主管，这是 什么 颜色？

zhǔguǎn: Zhè shì lǜsè. Zhè shì yí gè ānquán biāozhì.
主管：这是 绿色。这是 一个 安全 标志。

xuétú: Nà tā dàibiǎo shénme yìsi ya?
学徒：那它代表 什么 意思呀？

安全标志 4
Safety Signs

zhǔguǎn: Tā dàibiǎo de yìsi shì zhèlǐ shì ānquán tōngdào.
主管：它代表的意思是这里是安全通道。

译文 yìwén Text in English

Apprentice: Supervisor, what color is this?
Supervisor: It's green. It's a safety sign.
Apprentice: What does it mean then?
Supervisor: It means that here is a safe passage.

普通词语 pǔtōng cíyǔ General Vocabulary 04-04

1.	这	zhè	pron.	this
2.	颜色	yánsè	n.	color
3.	绿色	lǜsè	n.	green
4.	一	yī	num.	one
5.	那	nà	conj.	then, in that case
6.	它	tā	pron.	it
7.	代表	dàibiǎo	v.	represent, stand for
8.	意思	yìsi	n.	meaning
9.	呀	ya	part.	a variant of 啊 used after a word ending in a, e, i, o or ü
10.	这里	zhèlǐ	pron.	here

专业词语 zhuānyè cíyǔ Specialized Vocabulary 04-05

1.	安全标志	ānquán biāozhì	phr.	safety sign
	标志	biāozhì	n.	sign
2.	安全通道	ānquán tōngdào	phr.	safe passage
	通道	tōngdào	n.	passage, passageway access

B 04-06

xuétú: Zhǔguǎn, shénme shì ānquán biāozhì?
学徒：主管，什么是安全标志？

zhǔguǎn: Ānquán biāozhì shì yònglái biǎodá tèdìng de ānquán xìnxī de.
主管：安全标志是用来表达特定的安全信息的。

43

xuétú: Nà ānquán biāozhì bāohán nǎxiē ne?
学徒：那 安全 标志 包含 哪些 呢？

zhǔguǎn: Ānquán biāozhì bāohán zhǐshì biāozhì、jǐnggào biāozhì、jìnzhǐ biāozhì、jiùhù biāozhì děng.
主管：安全 标志 包含 指示 标志、警告 标志、禁止 标志、救护 标志 等。

译文 yìwén Text in English

Apprentice: Supervisor, what are safety signs?
Supervisor: They are used to indicate specific safety information.
Apprentice: What do safety signs include?
Supervisor: They include direction signs, warning signs, prohibition signs, first-aid signs, etc.

普通词语 pǔtōng cíyǔ General Vocabulary   🎧 04-07

1.	用来	yònglái	phr.	use
2.	表达	biǎodá	v.	express
3.	包含	bāohán	v.	include
4.	等	děng	part.	etc., and so on

专业词语 zhuānyè cíyǔ Specialized Vocabulary   🎧 04-08

1.	特定	tèdìng	adj.	specific
2.	信息	xìnxī	n.	information
3.	指示标志	zhǐshì biāozhì	phr.	direction sign
	指示	zhǐshì	v.	indicate
4.	警告标志	jǐnggào biāozhì	phr.	warning sign
	警告	jǐnggào	v.	warn
5.	禁止标志	jìnzhǐ biāozhì	phr.	prohibition sign
	禁止	jìnzhǐ	v.	prohibit
6.	救护标志	jiùhù biāozhì	phr.	first-aid sign
	救护	jiùhù	v.	give first-aid (to)

三、视听说　shì-tīng-shuō　Viewing, Listening and Speaking

观看介绍安全标志种类的视频，根据图片内容填写安全标志的含义所对应的序号，并模仿说出安全标志的含义。Watch the video introducing types of safety signs, fill in the serial numbers of the safety signs according to the pictures, and tell their meanings.

　　　gāoyā wēixiǎn　　　　ānquán tōngdào　　　　bìxū　pèidài ānquánmào　　　jìnzhǐ pāizhào
❶ 高压 危险　　❷ 安全 通道　　❸ 必须 佩戴 安全帽　　❹ 禁止 拍照

（　　）　　　（　　）　　　（　　）　　　（　　）

四、学以致用　xuéyǐzhìyòng　Practicing What You Have Learnt

观看介绍如何应用安全标志的视频，将场景与对应的安全标志连线。Watch the video introducing the application of safety signs, and match the scenes with the corresponding safety signs.

45

cāngkù
① 仓库

A. 当心叉车 Caution, fork lift trucks

chǎngqū dàolù
② 厂区 道路

B. 当心触电

shēngchǎn chējiān
③ 生产 车间

C. 当心夹手 Caution, nip hand

gōngzuòtái
④ 工作台

D. 禁止吸烟

第三部分 Part 3

课堂用语 Classroom Expressions

① 准备好了吗？ Zhǔnbèi hǎo le ma? Are you ready?
② 请打开书，翻到第十页。Qǐng dǎkāi shū, fāndào dì-shí yè. Please open your book and turn to page 10.

第四部分　Part 4　单元实训 Unit Practical Training

了解安全标志
Understanding Safety Signs

实训目的 Training purpose

通过本次实训，实训人员能够认识各种安全标志。
Through the training, the students will be able to know all kinds of safety signs.

实训组织 Training organization

实训人员进入车间，分成4组，各组对应一类安全标志，分别为警告标志、号令标志、救护标志、禁止标志。各小组寻找实地标志并进行知识竞赛。
The students enter the workshop and are divided into four groups, each of which corresponds to a type of safety signs, namely warning signs, direction signs, first-aid signs and prohibition signs. The groups search for field signs and carry out a knowledge contest.

实训步骤 Training steps

1. 教师讲解规则，宣布开始。各组在车间各个地方寻找属于自己小组的安全标志。
   The teacher explains the rules and kicks off the contest. Each group searches all parts of the workshop for its safety signs.
2. 各小组汇报找到的安全标志。
   All the teams report the safety signs they have found.
3. 安全标志知识大竞赛：各小组抢答竞猜看到这些标志可以做什么，不可以做什么。
   Safety signs knowledge contest: the groups answer and guess what they can/can't do when they see these signs.
4. 教师点评，实训结束。
   The teacher comments and the training ends.

第五部分　Part 5　单元小结 Unit Summary

cíyǔ 词语 Vocabulary

普通词语　General Vocabulary

1.	这	zhè	pron.	this
2	颜色	yánsè	n.	color
3.	绿色	lǜsè	n.	green
4.	一	yī	num.	one
5.	那	nà	conj.	then, in that case
6.	它	tā	pron.	it

47

词语 cíyǔ Vocabulary

7.	代表	dàibiǎo	v.	represent, stand for
8.	意思	yìsi	n.	meaning
9.	呀	ya	part.	*a variant of 啊 used after a word ending in a, e, i, o or ü*
10.	这里	zhèlǐ	pron.	here
11.	用来	yònglái	phr.	use
12.	表达	biǎodá	v.	express
13.	包含	bāohán	v.	include
14.	等	děng	part.	etc., and so on

专业词语　Specialized Vocabulary

1.	安全标志	ānquán biāozhì	phr.	safety sign
	标志	biāozhì	n.	sign
2.	安全通道	ānquán tōngdào	phr.	safe passage
	通道	tōngdào	n.	passage, passageway access
3.	特定	tèdìng	adj.	specific
4.	信息	xìnxī	n.	information
5.	指示标志	zhǐshì biāozhì	phr.	direction sign
	指示	zhǐshì	v.	indicate
6.	警告标志	jǐnggào biāozhì	phr.	warning sign
	警告	jǐnggào	v.	warn
7.	禁止标志	jìnzhǐ biāozhì	phr.	prohibition sign
	禁止	jìnzhǐ	v.	prohibit
8.	救护标志	jiùhù biāozhì	phr.	first-aid sign
	救护	jiùhù	v.	give first-aid (to)

补充专业词语　Supplementary Specialized Vocabulary

1.	三角形	sānjiǎoxíng	n.	triangle
2.	圆形	yuánxíng	n.	round, circle
3.	黄色	huángsè	n.	yellow
4.	黑色	hēisè	n.	black
5.	红色	hóngsè	n.	red

cíyǔ **词语** Vocabulary	6. 白底	bái dǐ	phr.	white background
	7. 边框	biānkuàng	n.	frame
	8. 横杠	héng gàng	phr.	horizontal bar
	9. 高压电	gāoyādiàn	n.	high-voltage electricity
	10. 拍照	pāi//zhào	v.	take a picture
	11. 吸烟	xī//yān	v.	smoke
	12. 当心	dāngxīn	v.	watch out
	13. 触电	chù//diàn	v.	get an electric shock
jùzi **句子** Sentences	1. 这是绿色。这是一个安全标志。 2. 安全标志是用来表达特定的安全信息的。 3. 安全标志包含指示标志、警告标志、禁止标志、救护标志等。			

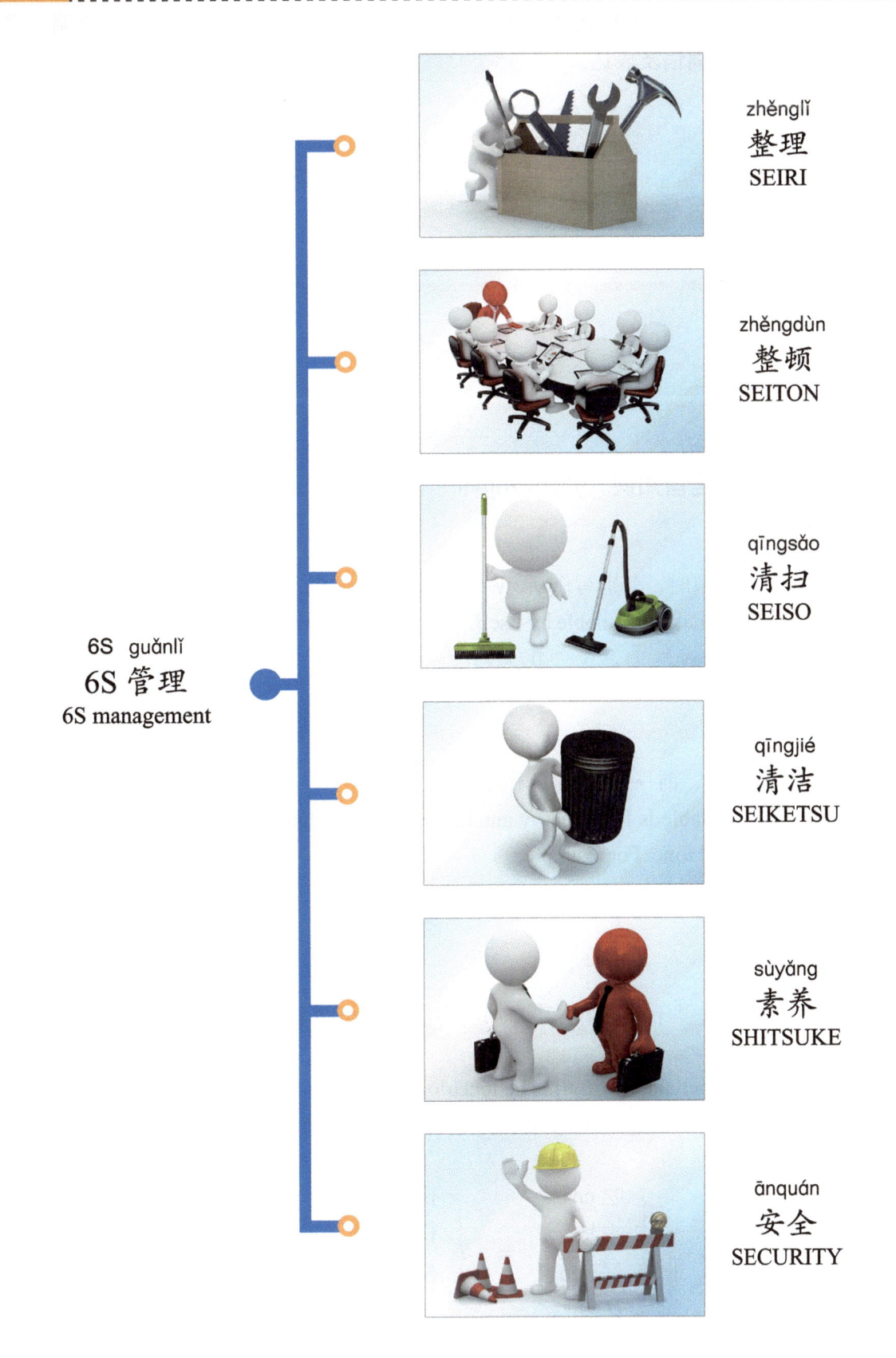

5

6S guǎnlǐ
6S 管理
6S Management

6S guǎnlǐ
6S 管理
6S management

- zhěnglǐ
  整理
  SEIRI

- zhěngdùn
  整顿
  SEITON

- qīngsǎo
  清扫
  SEISO

- qīngjié
  清洁
  SEIKETSU

- sùyǎng
  素养
  SHITSUKE

- ānquán
  安全
  SECURITY

51

> **题解　Introduction**
>
> 1. 学习内容：6S 管理的基本内容和理念、6S 管理的基本步骤。
>   Learning content: The basic content and ideas of 6S management, and the basic steps of 6S management
> 2. 知识目标：掌握 i、u、ü 单独构成音节时的拼写规则、三声变调和"不"的变调，掌握与 6S 管理相关的核心词语及表达。
>   Knowledge objectives: To master the spelling rules when the finals i, u, ü form independent syllables, the third-tone sandhi, the tone sandhi of "不", and acquire the core vocabulary and expressions related to 6S management
> 3. 技能目标：能完成 6S 管理任务。
>   Skill objective: To be able to complete the task of 6S management

第一部分　Part 1
语音　Phonetic Learning

一、语音知识　yǔyīn zhīshi　Knowledge about Phonetics

1. 拼写规则（1）Spelling rules (1)

i、u、ü 单独构成音节时，分别写作 yi、wu、yu。
When "i", "u" or "ü" makes a syllable by itself, the syllable is written as follows.

i → yi　　　　u → wu　　　　ü → yu

2. 三声变调　Third-tone sandhi

两个三声音节连读时，前一个三声声调读二声。例如：
When a third-tone syllable is followed by another third-tone syllable, the third tone in the first syllable is pronounced as the second tone. For example,

nǐ hǎo 读作 ní hǎo　　　　　　　　　　Fǎyǔ 读作 Fáyǔ

3. "不"的变调　Tone sandhi of "不"

"不"本调是第四声。"不"在第一声、第二声、第三声前面时，声调不变；在第四声前面时，读第二声。例如：
"不" is a fourth-tone syllable by itself. The tone doesn't change when "不" is followed by a first-tone, second-tone or third-tone syllable, but it becomes the second tone when "不" is followed by a fourth-tone syllable. For example,

不 bù + { 吃 chī / 来 lái / 好 hǎo / 是 shì } = { 不+吃　bù chī / 不+来　bù lái / 不+好　bù hǎo / 不+是　bú shì }

52

二、语音练习　yǔyīn liànxí　Pronunciation Drills

1. 读下面的词语，并在"bu"上边标上声调　Read the following words and add tone marks to "bu".

不喝 bu hē　　　　　不吃 bu chī　　　　　不多 bu duō

不学 bu xué　　　　　不想 bu xiǎng　　　　不小 bu xiǎo

不买 bu mǎi　　　　　不看 bu kàn　　　　　不去 bu qù

不对 bu duì　　　　　不累 bu lèi　　　　　不要 bu yào

不漂亮 bu piàoliang　　不客气 bu kèqi　　　　不上网 bu shàngwǎng

不新鲜 bu xīnxiān　　　不知道 bu zhīdào　　　不开门 bu kāimén

2. 读一读　Let's read.

① 整理 zhěnglǐ　　② 货架 huòjià　　③ 打扫 dǎsǎo　　④ 检查 jiǎnchá

⑤ 干净 gānjìng　　⑥ 整洁 zhěngjié　　⑦ 环境 huánjìng　　⑧ 物品 wùpǐn

⑨ 指定 zhǐdìng　　⑩ 区域 qūyù　　⑪ 管理 guǎnlǐ　　⑫ 扫地 sǎodì

第二部分　Part 2
课文　Texts

一、热身　rèshēn　Warm-up

1. 给词语选择对应的图片。Choose the corresponding picture for each word.

A.　　　B.　　　C.　　　D.

① 清洁工具 qīngjié gōngjù _____　　② 置物架 zhìwùjià _____
　　cleaning tool　　　　　　　　　　　　commodity shelf

③ 标签 biāoqiān _____　　　　　　④ 垃圾桶 lājītǒng _____
　　label　　　　　　　　　　　　　　　trash can

2. 观看介绍处理仓库作业现场的视频，将下列与 6S 管理相关的行为排序。**Watch the video introducing the processing of warehouse working site and sequence the following 6S management-related behaviors.**

① duīfàng zhěngqí
堆放 整齐
pile... in order

② dǎsǎo gānjìng
打扫 干净
clean up

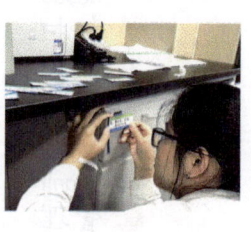

③ tiēshàng biāoqiān
贴上 标签
attach labels

④ ānquán jiǎnchá
安全 检查
give a security check

⑤ zhǐdìng wèizhì
指定 位置
designate a place

☐ → ☐ → ☐ → ☐ → ☐

二、课文　kèwén　Texts

A　05-01

xuétú: Zhǔguǎn, wǒmen jīntiān zuò shénme?
学徒：主管，我们今天做什么？

zhǔguǎn: Jīntiān wǒmen hěn máng. Wǒmen yào zhěnglǐ huòjià、dǎsǎo dìmiàn、dào lājī, hái yào jìnxíng ānquán jiǎnchá.
主管：今天我们很忙。我们要整理货架、打扫地面、倒垃圾，还要进行安全检查。

xuétú: Hǎo de. Zhèyàng wǒmen jiù yǒu yí gè gānjìng、zhěngjié、ānquán de gōngzuò huánjìng le.
学徒：好的。这样我们就有一个干净、整洁、安全的工作环境了。

6S 管理
6S Management

译文 yìwén Text in English

Apprentice: Supervisor, what are we going to do today?
Supervisor: We will be very busy today. We will tidy up the shelves, clean the floor, take out the trash, and give a security check.
Apprentice: All right. Then we will have a clean, neat and safe working environment.

普通词语 pǔtōng cíyǔ General Vocabulary 🎧 05-02

1.	我们	wǒmen	pron.	we, us
2.	很	hěn	adv.	very, so
3.	忙	máng	adj.	busy
4.	倒垃圾	dào lājī	phr.	take out the trash
	倒	dào	v.	dump, pour
	垃圾	lājī	n.	garbage, trash
5.	进行	jìnxíng	v.	conduct
6.	就	jiù	adv.	at once, right away
7.	了	le	part.	*used at the end of a sentence to indicate a change or the emergence of a new situation*

专业词语 zhuānyè cíyǔ Specialized Vocabulary 🎧 05-03

1.	整理	zhěnglǐ	v.	arrange, tidy up
2.	货架	huòjià	n.	goods shelves
3.	打扫	dǎsǎo	v.	sweep, clean
4.	地面	dìmiàn	n.	floor
5.	检查	jiǎnchá	v.	check
6.	干净	gānjìng	adj.	clean
7.	整洁	zhěngjié	adj.	clean and tidy, neat
8.	环境	huánjìng	n.	environment

B 🎧 05-04

xuétú: Zhǔguǎn, wǒ xiànzài yīnggāi zuò shénme?
学徒：主管，我现在应该做什么？

zhǔguǎn: Bǎ wùpǐn fàngdào zhǐdìng qūyù.
主管：把物品放到指定区域。

中文 + 机电一体化（初级）

xuétú: Zuótiān dàjiā wánchéngle ānquán péixùn, wǒmen jīntiān kěyǐ jìnrù chējiān le ma?
学徒：昨天大家完成了安全培训，我们今天可以进入车间了吗？

zhǔguǎn: Jìnrù chējiān qián, wǒmen yào xuéxí 6s guǎnlǐ, bǐrú sǎodì jiù shì yì zhǒng guǎnlǐ fāngfǎ.
主管：进入车间前，我们要学习6S管理，比如扫地就是一种管理方法。

译文 yìwén Text in English

Apprentice: Supervisor, what should I do now?
Supervisor: Put the items in the designated area.
Apprentice: We finished the safety training yesterday. Can we enter the workshop today?
Supervisor: Before entering the workshop, we need to learn 6S management, e.g. sweeping the floor is a management method.

普通词语 pǔtōng cíyǔ General Vocabulary　🎧 05-05

1.	现在	xiànzài	n.	now
2.	应该	yīnggāi	aux.	should
3.	把	bǎ	prep.	used to put the object before the verb
4.	放	fàng	v.	put, place
5.	到	dào	v.	used as a complement of a verb indicating the result of an action
6.	昨天	zuótiān	n.	yesterday
7.	完成	wán//chéng	v.	complete
8.	了	le	part.	used after a verb/an adjective to indicate the completion of an action/a change
9.	吗	ma	part.	used at the end of a question
10.	前	qián	n.	(in time) the past, the time before
11.	学习	xuéxí	v.	study, learn
12.	比如	bǐrú	v.	such as, for example
13.	种	zhǒng	m.	kind, type
14.	方法	fāngfǎ	n.	method, way

专业词语 zhuānyè cíyǔ Specialized Vocabulary　🎧 05-06

1.	物品	wùpǐn	n.	article, product
2.	指定	zhǐdìng	v.	designate

3.	区域	qūyù	n.	area
4.	培训	péixùn	v.	train
5.	管理	guǎnlǐ	v.	manage
6.	扫地	sǎo//dì	v.	sweep the floor

三、视听说　shì-tīng-shuō　Viewing, Listening and Speaking

观看介绍 6S 管理的视频，将图片所对应的 6S 管理的关键词序号填写在横线处，并模仿说出 6S 管理的关键词。Watch the video introducing 6S management, fill in the blanks with the serial numbers of the keywords of 6S management corresponding to the pictures, and tell the keywords of 6S management.

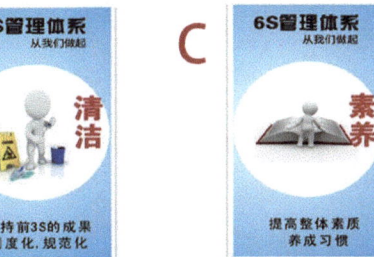

① 整理 zhěnglǐ　② 整顿 zhěngdùn　③ 清扫 qīngsǎo　④ 清洁 qīngjié　⑤ 安全 ānquán　⑥ 素养 sùyǎng

A. _____　B. _____　C. _____

D. _____　E. _____　F. _____

四、学以致用　xuéyǐzhìyòng　Practicing What You Have Learnt

观看介绍如何整顿的视频，并连线。Watch the video introducing the function of SEITON, and match them.

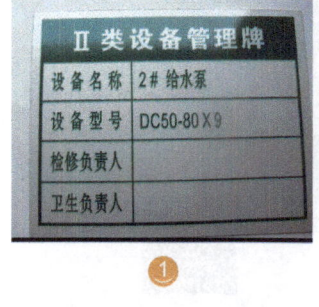

①

②

③

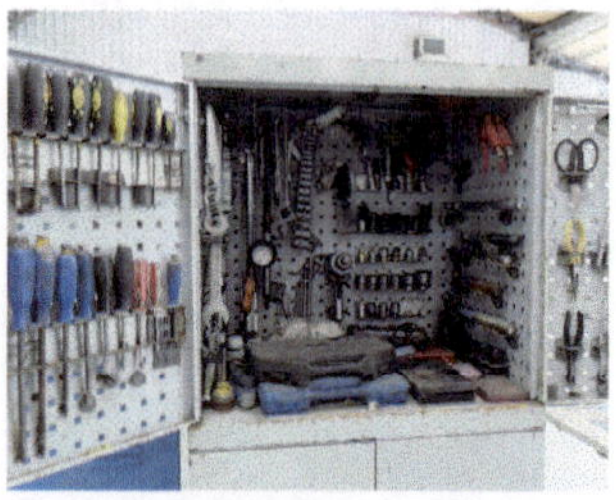

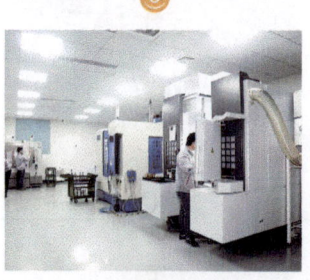

④

A.

B.

C.

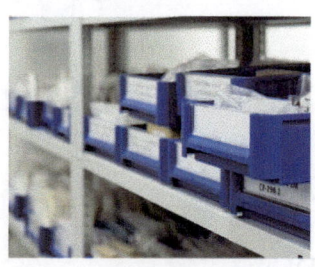

D.

第三部分 Part 3　课堂用语 Classroom Expressions

❶ 我明白了。Wǒ míngbai le. I see/understand.
❷ 我不懂。Wǒ bù dǒng. I don't know.

第四部分 Part 4　单元实训 Unit Practical Training

现场 6S 管理
On-Site 6S Management

实训目的 Training purpose
通过本次实训，实训人员能够了解 6S 管理。
Through the training, the students will be able to understand 6S management.

实训组织 Training organization
每组 6 人，选举一个组长。对培训教室进行分片包干，每组认领一项 6S 任务，取走任务卡片。
Students work in group of six and select a leader for each group. The classroom is divided into sections. Each group receives a 6S task and takes away the task card.

实训步骤 Training steps

❶ 教师讲解游戏规则，宣布开始。
　　The teacher explains the rules of the game and kicks off the game.
❷ 按认领的 6S 任务进行小组任务分配，每位实训人员完成后向组长汇报任务情况，并上交任务卡片。
　　Assign group tasks according to the 6S task received. After completing the task, each student reports to the group leader and hands in the task card.

任务一：整理，根据物品的性质决定物品的取舍。有用的留下来，无用的清除出去。
Task 1: SEIRI. Decide to keep or discard the items according to their nature. Keep the useful items and get rid of the useless ones.

任务二：整顿，将物品进行分类，按照机电类别将物品放置在不同的位置上。
Task 2: SEITON. Classify the items and put them in different locations based on the mechanical and electrical categories.

任务三：清洁，利用清洁工具对物品进行清洁。
Task 3: SEIKETSU. Use cleaning tools to clean the items.

任务四：清扫，利用清扫工具对培训中心进行清扫。
Task 4: SEISO. Clean up the training center using cleaning tools.

任务五：安全，安全小组负责寻找安全隐患并消除。

Task 5: SECURITY. The security group is responsible for looking for potential safety hazards and eliminating them.

任务六：素养，制订 6S 素养养成计划，并向全班公布。

Task 6: SHITSUKE. Develop the 6S SHITSUKE Cultivation Plan, and announce it to the class.

③ 小组组长根据任务完成情况进行总结（项目汇报法）。

Each group leader makes a summary based on the completion of the task (project reporting method).

④ 教师点评，实训结束。

The teacher comments, and the training ends.

第五部分　Part 5
单元小结　Unit Summary

词语 cíyǔ Vocabulary

普通词语　General Vocabulary

1.	我们	wǒmen	pron.	we, us
2.	很	hěn	adv.	very, so
3.	忙	máng	adj.	busy
4.	倒垃圾	dào lājī	phr.	take out the trash
	倒	dào	v.	dump, pour
	垃圾	lājī	n.	garbage, trash
5.	进行	jìnxíng	v.	conduct
6.	就	jiù	adv.	at once, right away
7.	了	le	part.	used at the end of a sentence to indicate a change or the emergence of a new situation
8.	现在	xiànzài	n.	now
9.	应该	yīnggāi	aux.	should
10.	把	bǎ	prep.	used to put the object before the verb
11.	放	fàng	v.	put, place
12.	到	dào	v.	used as a complement of a verb indicating the result of an action
13.	昨天	zuótiān	n.	yesterday
14.	完成	wán//chéng	v.	complete
15.	了	le	part.	used after a verb/an adjective to indicate the completion of an action/a change
16.	吗	ma	part.	used at the end of a question
17.	前	qián	n.	(in time) the past, the time before

词语 Vocabulary

18.	学习	xuéxí	v.	study, learn
19.	比如	bǐrú	v.	such as, for example
20.	种	zhǒng	m.	kind, type
21.	方法	fāngfǎ	n.	method, way

专业词语 Specialized Vocabulary

1.	整理	zhěnglǐ	v.	arrange, tidy up
2.	货架	huòjià	n.	goods shelves
3.	打扫	dǎsǎo	v.	sweep, clean
4.	地面	dìmiàn	n.	floor
5.	检查	jiǎnchá	v.	check
6.	干净	gānjìng	adj.	clean
7.	整洁	zhěngjié	adj.	clean and tidy, neat
8.	环境	huánjìng	n.	environment
9.	物品	wùpǐn	n.	article, product
10.	指定	zhǐdìng	v.	designate
11.	区域	qūyù	n.	area
12.	培训	péixùn	v.	train
13.	管理	guǎnlǐ	v.	manage
14.	扫地	sǎo//dì	v.	sweep the floor

补充专业词语 Supplementary Specialized Vocabulary

1.	整理	zhěnglǐ		SEIRI
2.	整顿	zhěngdùn		SEITON
3.	清洁	qīngjié		SEIKETSU
4.	清扫	qīngsǎo		SEISO
5.	安全	ānquán		SECURITY
6.	素养	sùyǎng		SHITSUKE
7.	清洁工具	qīngjié gōngjù	phr.	cleaning tool
8.	置物架	zhìwùjià	n.	commodity shelf
9.	垃圾桶	lājītǒng	n.	trash can
10.	堆放	duīfàng	v.	pile
11.	贴标签	tiē biāoqiān	phr.	attach labels

jùzi
句子
Sentences

1. 6S 管理包括整理、整顿、清扫、清洁、安全、素养。
2. 我们要整理货架、打扫地面、倒垃圾，还要进行安全检查。
3. 这样我们就有一个干净、整洁、安全的工作环境了。
4. 把物品放到指定区域。
5. 进入车间前，我们要学习 6S 管理。

6

Qiángōng gōngjù
钳工工具
Fitter's Tools

qiángōng gōngjù
钳工 工具
fitter's tools

luósīdāo
螺丝刀
screwdriver

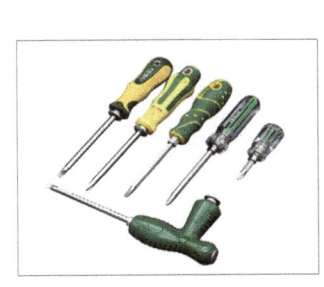

bānshou
扳手
wrench

shǒuqián
手钳
pliers

yàngchòng
样冲
sample punching pin

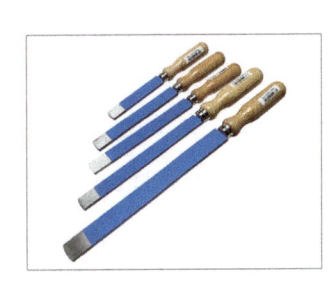

shǒuchuí
手锤
hand hammer

cuòdāo
锉刀
file

máhuāzuàn
麻花钻
twist drill

píngmiàn guādāo
平面 刮刀
flat scraper

63

> **题解　Introduction**
>
> 1. 学习内容：钳工工具的基本组成和使用方法。
>   Learning content: The basic composition and uses of fitter's tools
> 2. 知识目标：掌握以 i、u、ü 开头的韵母自成音节时的拼写规则，掌握与钳工工具相关的核心词语及表达。
>   Knowledge objectives: To master the spelling rules when the finals beginning with i, u, and ü form independent syllables, and acquire the core vocabulary and expressions related to fitter's tools
> 3. 技能目标：能使用钳工工具。
>   Skill objective: To be able to use fitter's tools

第一部分　Part 1　语音 Phonetic Learning

一、语音知识　yǔyīn zhīshi　Knowledge about Phonetics

拼写规则（2）　Spelling rules (2)

（1）以 i 开头的韵母自成音节时，除了 in、ing 前加 y 外，其他均是把 i 写作 y。

When "i" starts a syllable, it is written as "y", except in "in" and "ing", where "y" is added at the beginning.

ia→ya	ie→ye
iao→yao	iou→you
ian→yan	iang→yang
iong→yong	
in→yin	ing→ying

（2）以 u 开头的韵母自成音节时，u 写作 w。

When "u" starts a syllable, it is written as "w".

ua→wa	uo→wo
uai→wai	uei→wei
uan→wan	uen→wen
uang→wang	ueng→weng

（3）以 ü 开头的韵母自成音节时，ü 前面加上 y，去掉 ü 上的两点。

When "ü" starts a syllable, "y" is added in front of it and "ü" is written as "u".

üe→yue	üan→yuan	ün→yun

钳工工具
Fitter's Tools 6

二、语音练习 yǔyīn liànxí Pronunciation Drills

读一读 Let's read.

① gōngjù 工具
② táihǔqián 台虎钳
③ jùgōng 锯弓
④ qiángōngchuí 钳工锤
⑤ gāngjuǎnchǐ 钢卷尺
⑥ gōngzuòtái 工作台
⑦ píngtái 平台
⑧ gōngjùguì 工具柜
⑨ cúnchǔ 存储
⑩ luóshuān 螺栓
⑪ luómào 螺帽
⑫ shǒuqián 手钳

第二部分 Part 2
课文 Texts

一、热身 rèshēn Warm-up

1. 给词语选择对应的图片。**Choose the corresponding picture for each word.**

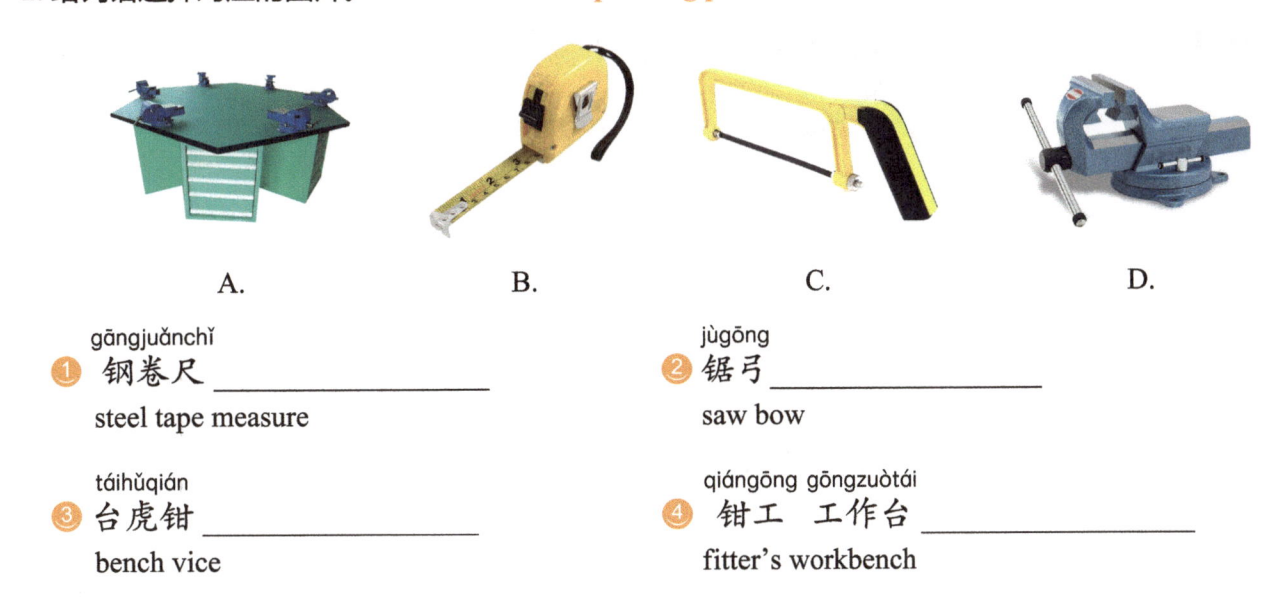

A.　　　B.　　　C.　　　D.

① gāngjuǎnchǐ 钢卷尺 _____
　steel tape measure

② jùgōng 锯弓 _____
　saw bow

③ táihǔqián 台虎钳 _____
　bench vice

④ qiángōng gōngzuòtái 钳工 工作台 _____
　fitter's workbench

2. 观看介绍钳工工具的视频，将钳工工具的名称的序号填入到空格里。**Watch the video introducing fitter's tools. Fill in the blanks with the serial numbers of the fitter's tools.**

rènshi qiángōng gōngjù
认识 钳 工 工具
understanding the fitter tools

中文 + 机电一体化（初级）

① shǒuqián 手钳 plier
② bānshou 扳手 wrench
③ luósīdāo 螺丝刀 screwdriver

A. →

B. →

C. →

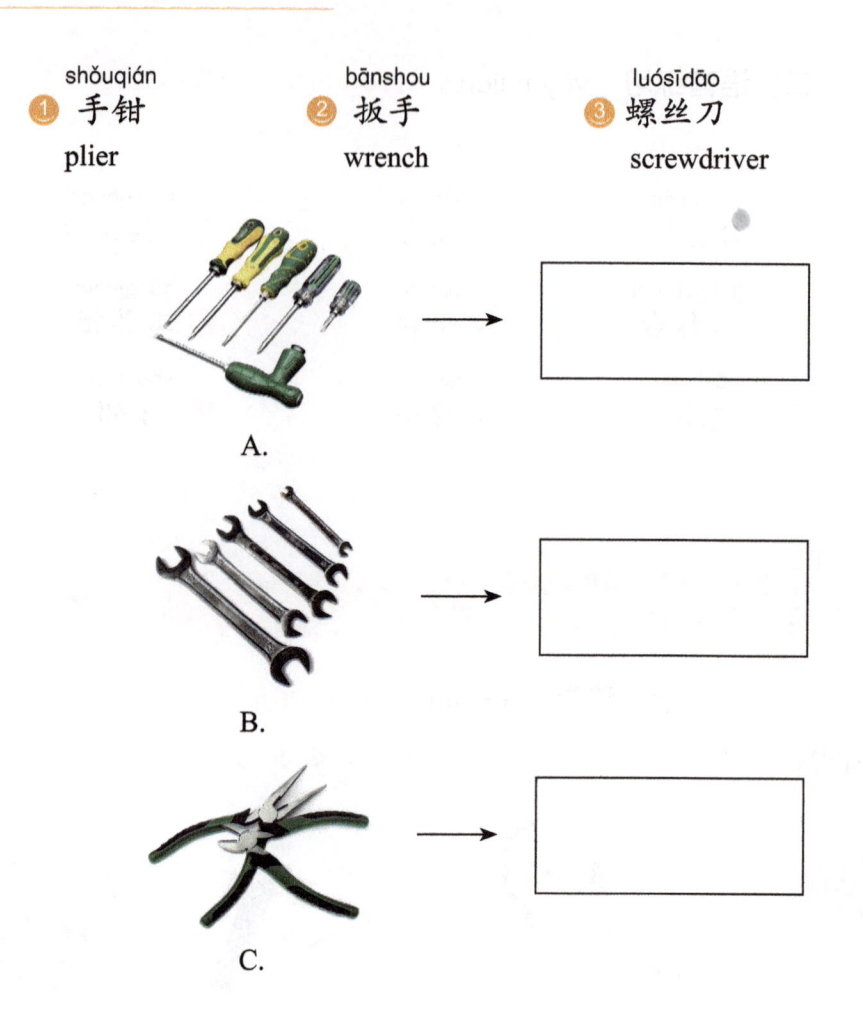

二、课文　kèwén　Texts

A　06-01

xuétú: Zhǔguǎn, qǐngwèn jīntiān yǒu shénme ānpái?
学徒：主管，请问今天有什么安排？

zhǔguǎn: Jīntiān xuéxí qiángōng gōngjù.
主管：今天学习钳工工具。

xuétú: Nǎxiē shì qiángōng gōngjù ne?
学徒：哪些是钳工工具呢？

zhǔguǎn: Qiángōng gōngjù bāokuò táihǔqián、jùgōng、qiángōngchuí、gāngjuǎnchǐ děng.
主管：钳工工具包括台虎钳、锯弓、钳工锤、钢卷尺等。

译文 yìwén Text in English

Apprentice: Supervisor, what's the plan for today?
Supervisor: Let's learn fitter's tools today.
Apprentice: What are fitter's tools?
Supervisor: They include a bench vice, saw bow, fitter's hammer, steel tape measure, etc.

钳工工具
Fitter's Tools 6

普通词语 pǔtōng cíyǔ General Vocabulary 🎧 06-02

1.	安排	ānpái	n./v.	arrangement; arrange

专业词语 zhuānyè cíyǔ Specialized Vocabulary 🎧 06-03

1.	工具	gōngjù	n.	tool
2.	台虎钳	táihǔqián	n.	bench vice
3.	锯弓	jùgōng	n.	saw bow
4.	钳工锤	qiángōngchuí	n.	fitter's hammer
5.	钢卷尺	gāngjuǎnchǐ	n.	steel tape measure

B 🎧 06-04

xuétú: Zhǔguǎn, qiángōng gōngzuòtái shì shénme?
学徒：主管，钳工 工作台是什么？

zhǔguǎn: Shì shǐyòng qiángōng gōngjù de píngtái.
主管：是使用 钳工 工具的平台。

xuétú: Nà gōngjùguì ne?
学徒：那工具柜呢？

zhǔguǎn: Gōngjùguì shì yònglái cúnchǔ gèzhǒng qiángōng gōngjù de.
主管：工具柜是用来存储各种 钳工 工具的。

译文 yìwén Text in English

Apprentice: Supervisor, what is a fitter's work bench?
Supervisor: It's a platform for using fitter's tools.
Apprentice: What is a tool cabinet?
Supervisor: It's used to store various fitter's tools.

普通词语 pǔtōng cíyǔ General Vocabulary 🎧 06-05

1.	使用	shǐyòng	v.	use
2.	各种	gèzhǒng	pron.	various, all kinds of
	各	gè	pron.	all, every

专业词语 zhuānyè cíyǔ Specialized Vocabulary 🎧 06-06

1.	工作台	gōngzuòtái	n.	workbench
2.	平台	píngtái	n.	platform
3.	工具柜	gōngjùguì	n.	tool cabinet
4.	存储	cúnchǔ	v.	store

67

三、视听说　shì-tīng-shuō　Viewing, Listening and Speaking

观看介绍钳工设备的视频，在横线处填写相应的钳工设备。**Watch the video introducing fitter's equipment, and fill in the blanks with corresponding fitter's equipment.**

qiángōng shèbèi
钳工设备
fitter's equipment

　　　shālúnjī　　　　　　　táihǔqián　　　　　　　qiángōngtái
A. 砂轮机　　　　　B. 台虎钳　　　　　　C. 钳工台
grinding machine　　　bench vice　　　　　fitter's work bench

❶ yòngyú ānzhuāng táihǔqián de shèbèi
用于 安装 台虎钳的设备 ＿＿＿＿＿＿
device for the installation of a bench vice

❷ yòngyú jiā chí gōngjiàn de shèbèi
用于夹持工件的设备 ＿＿＿＿＿＿
device for clamping workpieces

❸ yòngyú móxiāo gèzhǒng gōngjù de shèbèi
用于磨削各种工具的设备 ＿＿＿＿＿＿
device for grinding various tools

四、学以致用　xuéyǐzhìyòng　Practicing What You Have Learnt

观看介绍各种钳工工具作用的视频，然后根据实际情况选择合适的钳工工具。Watch the video introducing the functions of various fitter's tools, and then select the appropriate fitter's tools according to the actual situations.

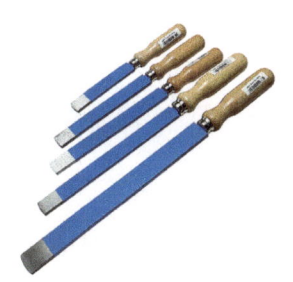

qiángōng gōngjù de zuòyòng
钳工工具的作用
functions of various fitter's tools

píngmiàn guādāo
A. 平面 刮刀
flat scraper

cuòdāo
B. 锉刀
file

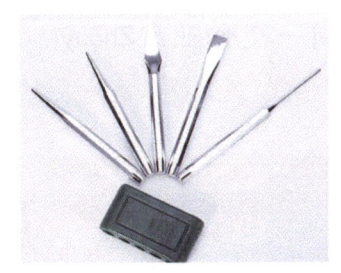

yàngchòng
C. 样冲
sample punching pin

shǒuchuí
D. 手锤
hand hammer

máhuāzuàn
E. 麻花钻
twist drill

huàxiàn shí xūyào de qiángōng gōngjù
❶ 划线 时 需要 的 钳工 工具 _____
tool for scribing

zànxiāo shí shǐyòng de qiángōng gōngjù
❷ 錾削 时 使用 的 钳工 工具 _____
tool for chiseling

cuòxiāo shí shǐyòng de qiángōng gōngjù
③ 锉削 时 使用 的 钳工 工具 _____
tool for filing

kǒng jiāgōng shí shǐyòng de qiángōng gōngjù
④ 孔 加工时 使用 的 钳工 工具 _____
tool for hole machining

guāxiāo shí shǐyòng de qiángōng gōngjù
⑤ 刮削 时 使用 的 钳工 工具 _____
tool for scraping

第三部分　Part 3　课堂用语 Classroom Expressions

① 现在做练习。Xiànzài zuò liànxí. Now it's time for exercises.
② 周一交作业。Zhōuyī jiāo zuòyè. Hand in your homework on Monday.

第四部分　Part 4　单元实训 Unit Practical Training

了解钳工工具及其使用方法
Understanding Fitter's Tools and Their Uses

实训目的 Training purpose

通过本次实训，实训人员能够认识各种钳工工具。
Through the training, the students will be able to know various fitter's tools.

实训组织 Training organization

实训人员进入车间，分成5组，每组对应一类钳工工具，分别用于划线、錾削、锉削、孔加工、刮削。认识各类钳工工具。
The students enter the workshop, and are divided into five groups, each of which respectively corresponds to a type of fitter's tools for scribing, chiseling, filing, hole machining, and scraping. Get to know these tools.

实训步骤 Training steps

① 教师讲解规则，宣布开始。每组实训人员在车间各个工作台学习如何使用五类钳工工具。
The teacher explains the rules and kicks off the training. Each group of students learn how to use five kinds of tools at various workbenches in the workshop.

② 各小组互换工具类别，确保每组实训人员学习到所有类别的钳工工具的使用方法。
Exchange types of tools in each group to ensure that every group of students can learn the uses of all

kinds of fitter's tools.

❸ 知识大竞赛。教师随机拿出钳工工具，实训人员说出它的名称和用途。
Knowledge contest. The teacher randomly takes out a fitter's tool, and the students tell its name and use.

❹ 教师点评，实训结束。
The teacher comments, and the training ends.

第五部分　Part 5　单元小结 Unit Summary

词语 Vocabulary (cíyǔ)

普通词语　General Vocabulary

1.	安排	ānpái	n./v.	arrangement; arrange
2.	使用	shǐyòng	v.	use
3.	各种	gèzhǒng	pron.	various, all kinds of
	各	gè	pron.	all, every

专业词语　Specialized Vocabulary

1.	工具	gōngjù	n.	tool
2.	台虎钳	táihǔqián	n.	bench vice
3.	锯弓	jùgōng	n.	saw bow
4.	钳工锤	qiángōngchuí	n.	fitter's hammer
5.	钢卷尺	gāngjuǎnchǐ	n.	steel tape measure
6.	工作台	gōngzuòtái	n.	workbench
7.	平台	píngtái	n.	platform
8.	工具柜	gōngjùguì	n.	tool cabinet
9.	存储	cúnchǔ	v.	store

补充专业词语　Supplementary Specialized Vocabulary

1.	旋入	xuánrù	phr.	screw in
2.	旋出	xuánchū	phr.	screw out
3.	螺栓	luóshuān	n.	screw bolt
4.	螺帽	luómào	n.	nut
5.	手钳	shǒuqián	n.	plier
6.	扳手	bānshou	n.	wrench
7.	螺丝刀	luósīdāo	n.	screwdriver

中文＋机电一体化（初级）

jùzi
句子
Sentences

1. 钳工工具包括台虎钳、锯弓、钳工锤、钢卷尺等。
2. 钳工工作台是使用钳工工具的平台。
3. 钳工工具柜是用来存储各种钳工工具的。

7

Cuòxiāo
锉削
Filing

cuòxiāo bùzhòu
锉削 步骤
steps of filing

quèrèn túzhǐ
确认图纸
confirm the drawing

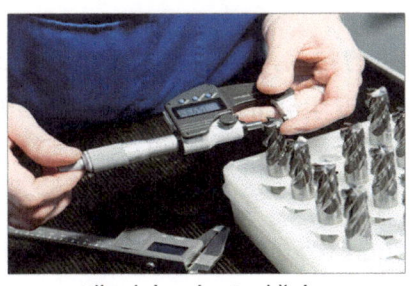

jiǎnchá máopī chǐcùn
检查毛坯尺寸
check the blank size

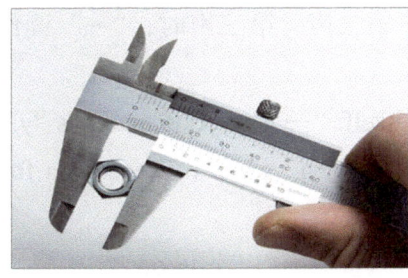

wánchéng jiāgōng hòu jìnxíng cèliáng
完成 加工后进行测量
measure it after finishing the process

quèdìng gōngjiàn máopī
确定 工件 毛坯
determine the workpiece blank

kāishǐ jiāgōng
开始加工
start processing

quèdìng chéngpǐn yǔ túzhǐ shìfǒu xiāngfú
确定 成品 与图纸是否 相符
confirm whether the finished product is consistent with the drawing

73

题解 Introduction

1. 学习内容：锉削工具、锉削的基本步骤。
   Learning content: The filing tools and the basic steps of filing
2. 知识目标：掌握 ü 或者以 ü 开头的韵母跟 j、q、x 相拼的拼写规则和"一"的变调，掌握与锉削相关的核心词语及表达。
   Knowledge objectives: To master the spelling rules for ü or finals starting with ü combined with j, q, and x, and the tone sandhi of "一", and acquire the core vocabulary and expressions related to filing
3. 技能目标：能使用锉削工具。
   Skill objective: To be able to use filing tools

第一部分 Part 1 语音 Phonetic Learning

一、语音知识 yǔyīn zhīshi Knowledge about Phonetics

1. 拼写规则（3） Spelling rules (3)

ü 或者以 ü 开头的韵母跟 j、q、x 相拼的时候，省略 ü 上边的两点，写成 ju、qu、xu、jue、que、xue、juan、quan、xuan、jun、qun、xun。跟 n、l 相拼的时候，ü 上边的两点不能省略，写成 nü、lü、lüe、nüe。

When "ü" or a final beginning with "ü" is combined with "j", "q" or "x", "ü" is written as "u" like in "ju", "qu", "xu", "jue", "que", "xue", "juan", "quan", "xuan", "jun", "qun", "xun". When combined with "n" or "l", the two dots above "ü" can not be removed. For example, "nü", "lü", "lüe", "nüe".

2. "一"的变调 Tone sandhi of "一"

数词"一"本调是第一声。"一"后边的音节是第一声、第二声、第三声时，"一"读作"yì"；"一"后边的音节是第四声时，"一"读作"yí"。例如：

The numeral "一" is pronounced as "yī" when it stands by itself. "一" is pronounced as "yì" when it precedes a first-tone, second-tone or third-tone syllable. It is read as "yí" when it precedes a fourth-tone syllable. For example,

一斤 yì jīn　　一台 yì tái　　一种 yì zhǒng　　一个 yí gè

二、语音练习 yǔyīn liànxí Pronunciation Drills

读一读 Let's read.

① cuòxiāo 锉削　② gōngjiàn 工件　③ jīnshǔ 金属　④ bǎncuò 板锉

74

⑤ sānjiǎo cuòdāo 三角 锉刀	⑥ yuán cuòdāo 圆 锉刀	⑦ cuòshuā 锉刷	⑧ máocì 毛刺
⑨ qùchú 去除	⑩ tiěxiè 铁屑	⑪ biǎomiàn 表面	⑫ zuòyòng 作用

第二部分　Part 2
课文　Texts

一、热身　rèshēn　Warm-up

1. 给词语选择对应的图片。 Choose the corresponding picture for each word.

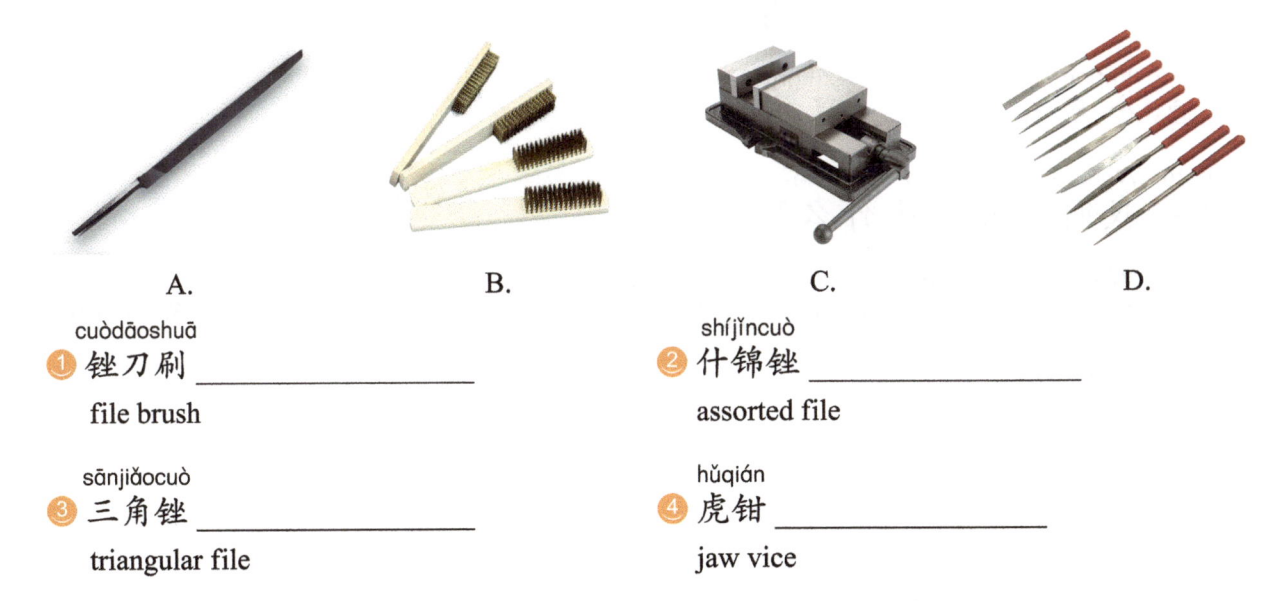

A.　　B.　　C.　　D.

① cuòdāoshuā
锉刀刷 _____
file brush

② shíjǐncuò
什锦锉 _____
assorted file

③ sānjiǎocuò
三角锉 _____
triangular file

④ hǔqián
虎钳 _____
jaw vice

2. 观看介绍锉削基本步骤的视频，根据图片内容选择相应的步骤序号，并模仿说出锉削的步骤。
Watch the video introducing the basic filing steps, choose the corresponding serial numbers of the steps according to the picture, and talk about the filing steps.

cuòxiāo jīběn bùzhòu
锉削 基本 步骤
basic filing steps

① jiājǐn gōngjiàn
夹紧 工件
clamp the workpiece

② cuòxiāo píngmiàn, qùchú máocì
锉削 平面，去除毛刺
file the surface to deburr

③ qīngjié cuòdāo
清洁 锉刀
clean the file

中文 + 机电一体化（初级）

(　　)　　　　　　　(　　)　　　　　　　(　　)

二、课文　kèwén　Texts

A 07-01

xuétú: Zhǔguǎn, jīntiān jǐ yuè jǐ hào?
学徒：主管，今天几月几号？

zhǔguǎn: Jīntiān liùyuè yī hào, xīngqīyī.
主管：今天 6 月 1 号，星期一。

xuétú: Wǒmen jīntiān xuéxí shénme?
学徒：我们今天学习什么？

zhǔguǎn: Wǒmen jīntiān xuéxí cuòxiāo. Cuòxiāo jiù shì cóng gōngjiàn biǎomiàn cuòdiào duōyú de jīnshǔ.
主管：我们今天学习锉削。锉削就是从工件表面锉掉多余的金属。

译文 yìwén Text in English

Apprentice: Supervisor, what's the date today?
Supervisor: It's Monday, June 1st.
Apprentice: What are we going to learn today?
Supervisor: We are going to learn filing. It is to remove excess metal from the workpiece surface.

普通词语　pǔtōng cíyǔ General Vocabulary   07-02

1.	几	jǐ	pron.	how many, what
2.	月	yuè	n.	month
3.	号	hào	m.	(usually used after numerals) an ordinal number for a date of a month
4.	六月	liùyuè	n.	June
5.	星期一	xīngqīyī	n.	Monday
6.	从	cóng	prep.	from
7.	表面	biǎomiàn	n.	surface
8.	掉	diào	v.	used after some verbs to indicate the result of an action

76

7 锉削 Filing

| 9. | 多余 | duōyú | adj. | excess, redundant, superfluous |

专业词语 zhuānyè cíyǔ Specialized Vocabulary 🎧 07-03

1.	锉削	cuòxiāo	v.	file
	锉	cuò	v.	make smooth with a file
	削	xiāo	v.	pare with a knife, whittle
2.	工件	gōngjiàn	n.	workpiece
3.	金属	jīnshǔ	n.	metal

B 🎧 07-04

xuétú: Zhǔguǎn, cuòxiāo yào shǐyòng nǎxiē gōngjù?
学徒：主管，锉削要使用哪些工具？

zhǔguǎn: Wǒmen xūyào bǎncuò、sānjiǎo cuòdāo hé yuán cuòdāo.
主管：我们需要板锉、三角锉刀和圆锉刀。

xuétú: Nà cuòxiāo de zuòyòng shì shénme?
学徒：那锉削的作用是什么？

zhǔguǎn: Zhǔyào shì qùchú gōngjiàn de máocì.
主管：主要是去除工件的毛刺。

译文 yìwén Text in English

Apprentice: Supervisor, what tools do we use for filing?
Supervisor: We need flat files, triangular files and round files.
Apprentice: What is the function of filing?
Supervisor: It is mainly to remove the burrs of the workpiece.

普通词语 pǔtōng cíyǔ General Vocabulary 🎧 07-05

| 1. | 需要 | xūyào | v. | need |
| 2. | 作用 | zuòyòng | n. | function |

专业词语 zhuānyè cíyǔ Specialized Vocabulary 🎧 07-06

1.	板锉	bǎncuò	n.	flat file
2.	三角锉刀	sānjiǎo cuòdāo	phr.	triangular file
3.	圆锉刀	yuán cuòdāo	phr.	round file
4	去除	qùchú	v.	remove, get rid of
5.	毛刺	máocì	n.	burr

77

三、视听说　shì-tīng-shuō　Viewing, Listening and Speaking

观看介绍锉削过程的视频，将锉削的步骤排序。Watch the video introducing the process of filing and sequence the steps of filing.

完整 的 锉削 步骤
wánzhěng de cuòxiāo bùzhòu
complete steps of filing

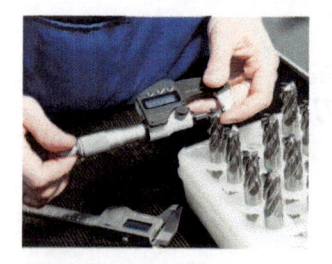

① jiǎnchá máopī chǐcùn
检查 毛坯 尺寸
check the size of the blank

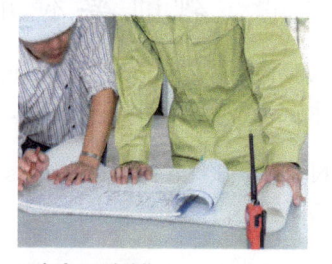

② quèrèn túzhǐ
确认 图纸
confirm the drawing

③ quèrèn gōngjiàn máopī
确认 工件 毛坯
confirm the workpiece blank

④ jiāgōng
加工
process

⑤ quèdìng chéngpǐn yǔ túzhǐ shìfǒu xiāngfú
确定 成品 与 图纸 是否 相符
confirm whether the finished product is consistent with the drawing

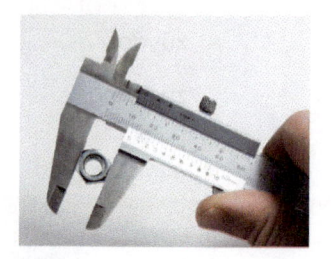

⑥ cèliáng
测量
measure

☐ → ☐ → ☐ → ☐ → ☐ → ☐

四、学以致用　xuéyǐzhìyòng　Practicing What You Have Learnt

观看介绍锉削工具作用的视频，然后根据实际情况将工件与用到的相应锉刀连线。
Watch the video introducing the role of filing tools, then match the workpieces with the corresponding files according to the actual situations.

sānjiǎoxíng kǒng gōngjiàn
① 三角形 孔 工件
workpieces with triangular holes

pǔtōng gōngjiàn
② 普通 工件
common workpieces

yuánxíng kǒng gōngjiàn
③ 圆形 孔 工件
workpieces with round holes

bǎncuò
A. 板锉
flat file

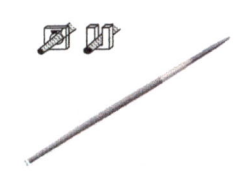

yuáncuò
B. 圆锉
round file

sānjiǎocuò
C. 三角锉
triangular file

第三部分　Part 3　课堂用语 Classroom Expressions

❶ 最近学习怎么样？　Zuìjìn xuéxí zěnmeyàng? How have you been studying lately?
❷ 你有事吗？　Nǐ yǒu shì ma? Can I help you?/What's up?

第四部分　Part 4　单元实训 Unit Practical Training

了解锉削工具及其使用方法
Understanding Filing Tools and Their Uses

实训目的 Training purpose

通过本次实训，实训人员能够掌握锉削工具的使用方法。

Through the training, the students will be able to master the uses of filing tools.

实训组织 Training organization

实训人员进入车间，分成 4 组，每组对应一类锉削工具，即板锉、圆锉、三角锉、异形锉刀。学习如何使用各类锉削工具。

The students enter the workshop, and are divided into four groups, each of which corresponds to a type of filing tools, namely a flat file, a round file, a triangular file and a special-shaped file. Learn how to use all kinds of filing tools.

实训步骤 Training steps

❶ 教师讲解规则，宣布开始。各组实训人员在车间各个工作台学习如何使用各类锉削工具。

The teacher explains the rules and kicks off the training. Each group of students learn to use various kinds of filing tools at various workbenches in the workshop.

❷ 小组互换工具类别，确保每组实训人员学习到所有类别的锉削工具的使用方法。

Exchange types of tools in each group to ensure that every group of students can learn the use of all kinds of filing tools.

❸ 知识大竞赛。教师随机拿出锉削工具，实训人员说出它的名称和用途。

Knowledge contest. The teacher randomly takes out a filing tool, and the students tell its name and use.

❹ 教师点评，实训结束。

The teacher comments, and the training ends.

第五部分 Part 5 单元小结 Unit Summary

词语 Vocabulary (cíyǔ)

普通词语 General Vocabulary

1.	几	jǐ	pron.	how many, what
2.	月	yuè	n.	month
3.	号	hào	m.	(usually used after numerals) an ordinal number for a date of a month
4.	六月	liùyuè	n.	June
5.	星期一	xīngqīyī	n.	Monday
6.	从	cóng	prep.	from
7.	表面	biǎomiàn	n.	surface
8.	掉	diào	v.	used after some verbs to indicate the result of an action
9.	多余	duōyú	adj.	excess, redundant, superfluous
10.	需要	xūyào	v.	need
11.	作用	zuòyòng	n.	function

专业词语 Specialized Vocabulary

1.	锉削	cuòxiāo	v.	file
	锉	cuò	v.	make smooth with a file
	削	xiāo	v.	pare with a knife, whittle
2.	工件	gōngjiàn	n.	workpiece
3.	金属	jīnshǔ	n.	metal
4.	板锉	bǎncuò	n.	flat file
5.	三角锉刀	sānjiǎo cuòdāo	phr.	triangular file
6.	圆锉刀	yuán cuòdāo	phr.	round file
7	去除	qùchú	v.	remove, get rid of
8.	毛刺	máocì	n.	burr

补充专业词语 Supplementary Specialized Vocabulary

1.	锉刷	cuòshuā	n.	file brush
2.	铁屑	tiěxiè	n.	iron filings

句子 Sentences (jùzi)

1. 锉削就是从工件表面锉掉多余的金属。
2. 锉削要使用板锉、三角锉刀和圆锉刀等工具。
3. 锉削的作用主要是去除工件的毛刺。

8

Huàxiàn yǔ jùxiāo
划线与锯削
Scribing and Sawing

jùxiāo de jīběn bùzhòu
锯削 的 基本 步骤
basic steps of sawing

yòng kàotiě gùdìng gōngjiàn
用 靠铁 固定 工件
fixing the workpiece with a cast iron angle plate

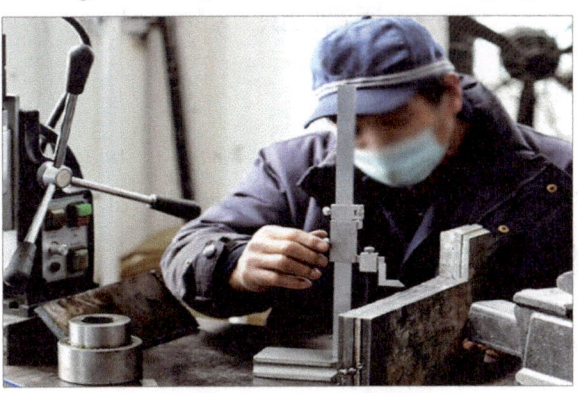

yòng gāodùchǐ huàxiàn
用 高度尺 划线
scribing with a height gauge

yòng jùgōng jùtiáo jùgē gōngjiàn
用 锯弓 锯条 锯割 工件
using a saw bow and saw blade to saw the workpiece

83

> **题解　Introduction**
>
> 1. 学习内容：划线和锯削工具、划线和锯削的基本步骤。
>   Learning content: The scribing and sawing tools, and the basic steps of scribing and sawing
> 2. 知识目标：掌握 iou、uei、uen 前面有声母时的拼写规则和"儿化"的基本知识，掌握与划线和锯削相关的核心词语及表达。
>   Knowledge objectives: To master the spelling rules when *iou, uei,* and *uen* are preceded by initials, and the basic knowledge of *erhua*, and acquire the core vocabulary and expressions related to scribing and sawing
> 3. 技能目标：能进行划线和锯削的实际操作。
>   Skill objective: To be able to perform practical operations of scribing and sawing

第一部分　Part 1

语音　Phonetic Learning

一、语音知识　yǔyīn zhīshi　Knowledge about Phonetics

1. 拼写规则（4）Spelling rules (4)

iou、uei、uen 前面有声母时，写成 iu、ui、un。例如：

"iou", "uei" and "uen" are written as "iu", "ui" and "un" after initials. For example,

n + iou → n + iu → niu

g + uei → g + ui → gui

l + uen → l + un → lun

2. 儿化　*Erhua*

卷舌元音 er 与其他韵母结合，使韵母带上卷舌色彩，这种现象称为"儿化"，卷舌的韵母称为"儿化韵"。"儿化"具有区别词义、区分词性和表示细小、轻松或亲切、喜爱的感情色彩的作用。儿化时，"儿"与前面的韵母读成一个音节。拼写时在前面韵母末尾加上"r"，汉字写法是在原来的汉字后边加"儿"。例如：

The combination of a retroflex vowel "er" with a final is called "*erhua*", and the final is called "*erhua* final". *Erhua* is used to discriminate word meanings and parts of speech, and express subtle, relaxed, or affectionate emotions. The "*er*" at the end is pronounced together with the syllable before it. In spelling, an "r" is added to the end of the syllable before it, and "儿" is added to the end of the original Chinese character. For example,

nǎ + er → nǎr（哪儿）

zhè + er → zhèr（这儿）

8 划线与锯削 Scribing and Sawing

二、语音练习 yǔyīn liànxí Pronunciation Drills

读一读 Let's read.

① huàxiàn 划线
② jùxiāo 锯削
③ jùgōng 锯弓
④ jùtiáo 锯条
⑤ huàguī 划规
⑥ kàotiě 靠铁
⑦ gāodùchǐ 高度尺
⑧ jùgē 锯割
⑨ xǐhuan 喜欢
⑩ dòngshǒu 动手
⑪ rènwu 任务
⑫ chǐcùn 尺寸

第二部分 Part 2 课文 Texts

一、热身 rèshēn Warm-up

1. 给词语选择对应的图片。Choose the corresponding picture for each word.

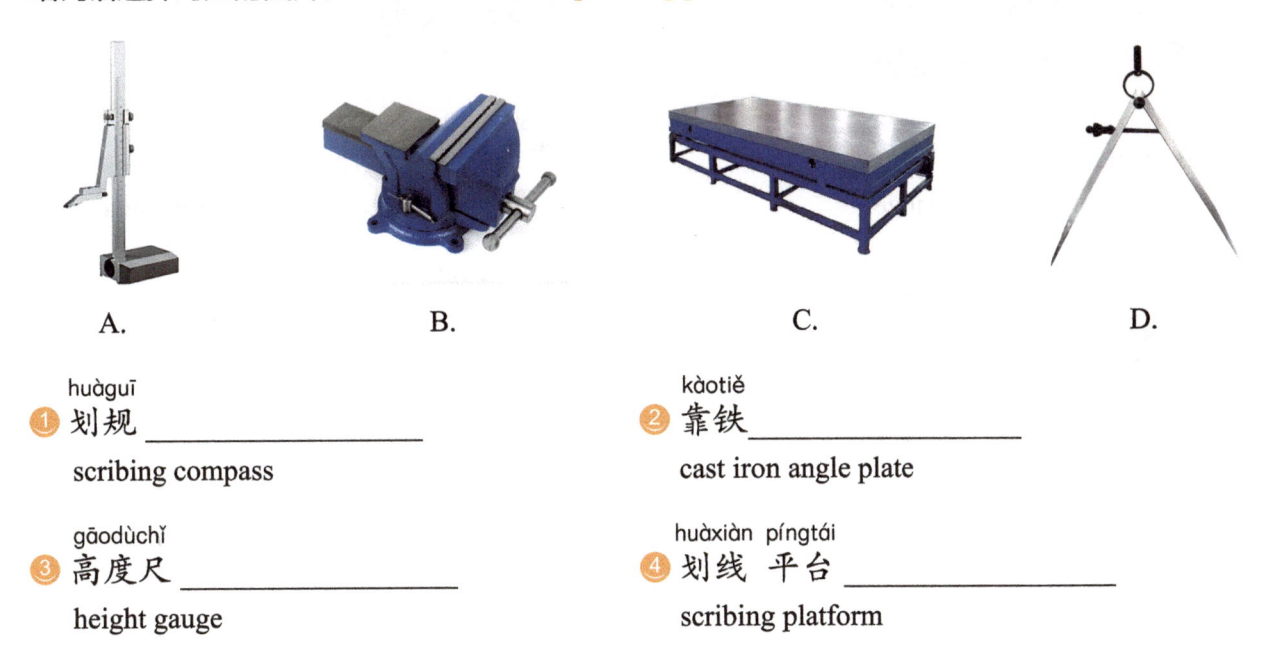

A. B. C. D.

① huàguī 划规 _____
scribing compass

② kàotiě 靠铁 _____
cast iron angle plate

③ gāodùchǐ 高度尺 _____
height gauge

④ huàxiàn píngtái 划线 平台 _____
scribing platform

2. 观看介绍锯削基本步骤的视频，将锯削的基本步骤排序。Watch the video introducing the basic steps of sawing and sequence these steps.

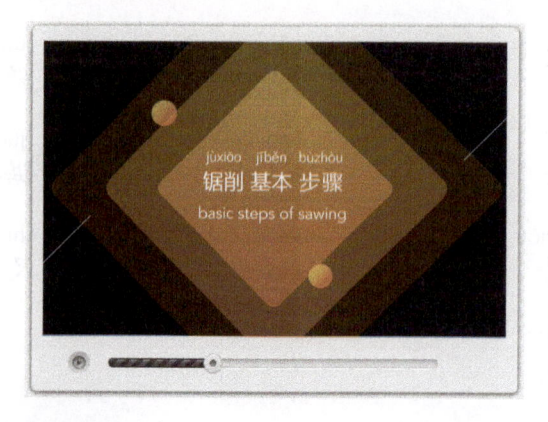

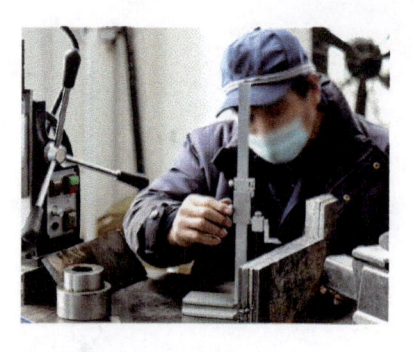

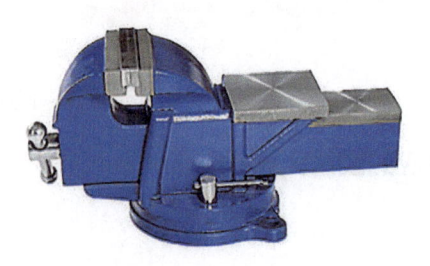

jùxiāo jīběn bùzhòu
锯削 基本 步骤
basic steps of sawing

yòng gāodùchǐ huàxiàn
❶ 用 高度尺 划线
scribing with a height gauge

yòng kàotiě gùdìng gōngjiàn
❷ 用 靠铁 固定 工件
fixing the workpiece with a cast iron angle plate

jùgē gōngjiàn
❸ 锯割 工件
sawing the workpiece

□ → □ → □

二、课文　kèwén　Texts

A　08-01

xuétú: Zhǔguǎn, wǒ hěn xǐhuan dòngshǒu cāozuò de xuéxí rènwu.
学徒：主管，我很喜欢 动手 操作的学习任务。

zhǔguǎn: Hěn hǎo! Wǒmen jīntiān lái xuéxí huàxiàn hé jùxiāo.
主管：很好！我们今天来学习划线和锯削。

8 划线与锯削
Scribing and Sawing

xuétú: Shénme shì huàxiàn hé jùxiāo?
学徒：什么 是 划线和 锯削？

zhǔguǎn: Gōngjiàn biǎomiàn cuòxiāo wánchéng hòu, yào ànzhào chǐcùn zài gōngjiàn biǎomiàn
主管：工件 表面 锉削 完成 后，要 按照 尺寸 在 工件 表面
huàxiàn, ránhòu yánzhe huàhǎo de xiàn jùkāi gōngjiàn.
划线，然后 沿着 画好 的 线 锯开 工件。

译文 yìwén Text in English

Apprentice: Supervisor, I like hands-on learning tasks very much.
Supervisor: Great! Today we are going to learn scribing and sawing.
Apprentice: What are scribing and sawing?
Supervisor: After filing the workpiece surface, it's necessary to scribe the workpiece surface according to the size and then saw it along the scribed line.

普通词语 pǔtōng cíyǔ General Vocabulary   08-02

1.	喜欢	xǐhuan	v.	like
2.	动手	dòng//shǒu	v.	do, get to work
3.	任务	rènwu	n.	task
4.	来	lái	v.	do (used a substitute for a more specific verb. e.g., to bring or to have)
5.	按照	ànzhào	prep.	according to
6.	尺寸	chǐcùn	n.	size
7.	然后	ránhòu	conj.	then, afterwards
8.	沿着	yánzhe	phr.	along
9.	画	huà	v.	draw, paint
10.	线	xiàn	n.	line
11.	开	kāi	v.	open

专业词语 zhuānyè cíyǔ Specialized Vocabulary   08-03

1.	操作	cāozuò	v.	operate
2.	划线	huà//xiàn	v.	mark lines
3.	锯削	jùxiāo	v.	saw
	锯	jù	v.	saw

B 🎧 08-04

xuétú: Zhǔguǎn, jùxiāo xūyào shǐyòng shénme gōngjù?
学徒：主管，锯削需要使用什么工具？

zhǔguǎn: Xūyào shǐyòng jùgōng hé jùtiáo.
主管：需要使用锯弓和锯条。

xuétú: Nà zěnme jìnxíng jùxiāo ne?
学徒：那怎么进行锯削呢？

zhǔguǎn: Shǐyòng jùgōng yánzhe huàhǎo de xiàn jùkāi gōngjiàn.
主管：使用锯弓沿着画好的线锯开工件。

译文 yìwén Text in English

Apprentice: Supervisor, what tools do we use for sawing?
Supervisor: We need to use saw bows and saw blades.
Apprentice: How do we saw then?
Supervisor: Saw the workpiece with the saw bow along the scribed line.

普通词语 pǔtōng cíyǔ General Vocabulary   🎧 08-05

| 1. | 怎么 | zěnme | pron. | how |

专业词语 zhuānyè cíyǔ Specialized Vocabulary   🎧 08-06

| 1. | 锯条 | jùtiáo | n. | saw blade |

三、视听说 shì-tīng-shuō Viewing, Listening and Speaking

观看介绍划线步骤的视频，根据图片内容选择相应的步骤序号，并模仿说出划线的步骤。**Watch the video introducing the steps of scribing, choose the corresponding serial numbers of the steps according to the picture, and tell the steps of scribing.**

huàxiàn de zhǔyào bùzhòu
划线的主要步骤
main steps of scribing

8 划线与锯削
Scribing and Sawing

① 用 划规 划线
yòng huàguī huàxiàn
scribing with a scribing compass

② 用 靠铁 固定 工件
yòng kàotiě gùdìng gōngjiàn
fixing the workpiece with a cast iron angle plate

③ 调节 高度尺
tiáojié gāodùchǐ
adjusting the height gauge

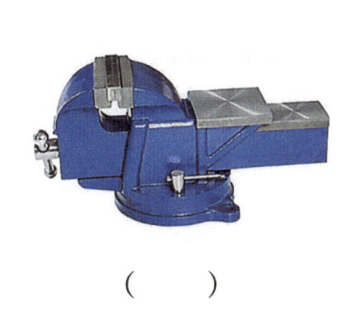

(　)　　(　)　　(　)

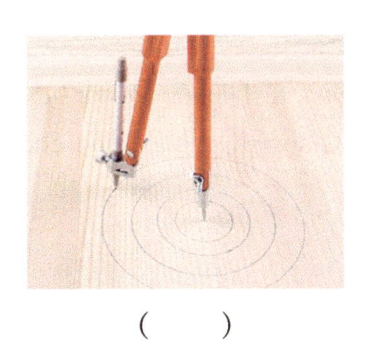

四、学以致用　xuéyǐzhìyòng　Practicing What You Have Learnt

观看介绍划线和锯削工具作用的视频，然后根据实际情况选择合适的工具。**Watch the video introducing the functions of scribing and sawing tools, and choose the appropriate tools according to the actual situations.**

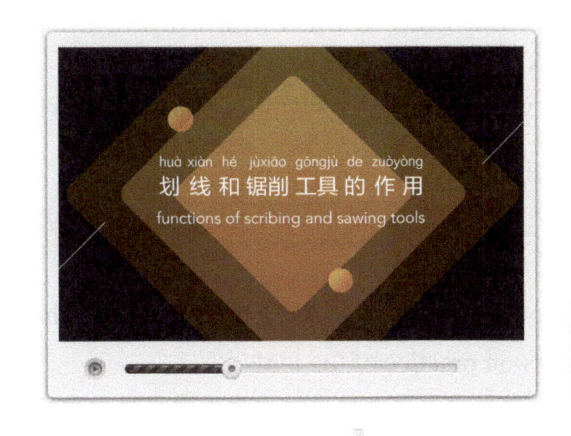

划线和锯削工具的作用
huà xiàn hé jùxiāo gōngjù de zuòyòng
functions of scribing and sawing tools

A. 　　B. 　　C. 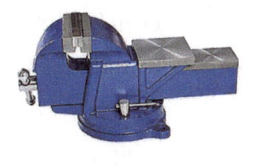　　D. 　　E.

① 操作 平台 _____
cāozuò píngtái
operating platform

② 测量 划线 尺寸 _____
cèliáng huàxiàn chǐcùn
measuring the scribing size

③ 划线 _____
huàxiàn
scribing

④ 固定 工件 _____
gùdìng gōngjiàn
fixing the workpiece

89

⑤ 锯割 工件 _____
　jùgē gōngjiàn
sawing the workpiece

第三部分　Part 3　课堂用语 Classroom Expressions

❶ 请问，图书馆在哪儿？　Qǐngwèn, túshūguǎn zài nǎr? Excuse me, where's the library?

❷ 请问，这个用中文怎么说？　Qǐngwèn, zhège yòng Zhōngwén zěnme shuō? Excuse me, how do you say it in Chinese?

第四部分　Part 4　单元实训 Unit Practical Training

了解划线与锯削的工具及其使用方法
Understanding Scribing and Sawing Tools and Their Uses

实训目的 Training purpose

通过本次实训，实训人员能够认识划线与锯削的工具，并了解其使用方法。

Through the training, the students will be able to know the scribing and sawing tools and their uses.

实训组织 Training organization

实训人员分组，每组 4～6 人，进入车间，进行图片与工具迅速配对活动以及工具的实际操作练习。

The students are divided into groups of 4-6. After they enter the workshop, they quickly match the pictures with the tools, and have a hands-on practice of the tools.

实训步骤 Training steps

❶ 教师讲解游戏规则，宣布根据图片找工具活动开始。

　The teacher explains the rules of the game, and announces the activity of finding tools based on the pictures starts.

❷ 各组 2 名或 3 名实训人员举起工具名称的图片，另 2 名或 3 名实训人员迅速找到相应的工具。

　Two or three students in each group hold up the pictures with the names of the tools, and the other two or three students find the corresponding tools quickly.

❸ 教师讲解划线和锯削工具的使用方法。

　The teacher explains the uses of scribing and sawing tools.

❹ 实训人员进行划线及锯削工具的实际操作。

　The students use the scribing and sawing tools.

❺ 教师示范讲解并点评，实训结束。
The teacher makes a demonstration and comments, and the training ends.

第五部分　Part 5　单元小结　Unit Summary

cíyǔ 词语 Vocabulary

普通词语　General Vocabulary

1.	喜欢	xǐhuan	v.	like
2.	动手	dòng//shǒu	v.	do, get to work
3.	任务	rènwu	n.	task
4.	来	lái	v.	do (used a substitute for a more specific verb. e.g., to bring or to have)
5.	按照	ànzhào	prep.	according to
6.	尺寸	chǐcùn	n.	size
7.	然后	ránhòu	conj.	then, afterwards
8.	沿着	yánzhe	phr.	along
9.	画	huà	v.	draw, paint
10.	线	xiàn	n.	line
11.	开	kāi	v.	open
12.	怎么	zěnme	pron.	how

专业词语　Specialized Vocabulary

1.	操作	cāozuò	v.	operate
2.	划线	huà//xiàn	v.	mark lines
3.	锯削	jùxiāo	v.	saw
	锯	jù	v.	saw
4.	锯条	jùtiáo	n.	saw blade

补充专业词语　Supplementary Specialized Vocabulary

1.	划规	huàguī	n.	scribing compass
2.	靠铁	kàotiě	n.	cast iron angle plate
3.	高度尺	gāodùchǐ	n.	height gauge
4.	锯割	jùgē	v.	saw

jùzi
句子
Sentences

1. 工件表面锉削完成后,要按照尺寸在工件表面划线,然后沿着画好的线锯开工件。
2. 锯削需要使用锯弓和锯条等工具。
3. 怎么进行锯削呢?使用锯弓沿着画好的线锯开工件。

9

Túzhǐ
图纸
Drawings

língjiàntú de gòuchéng
零件图的 构成
components of detail drawings

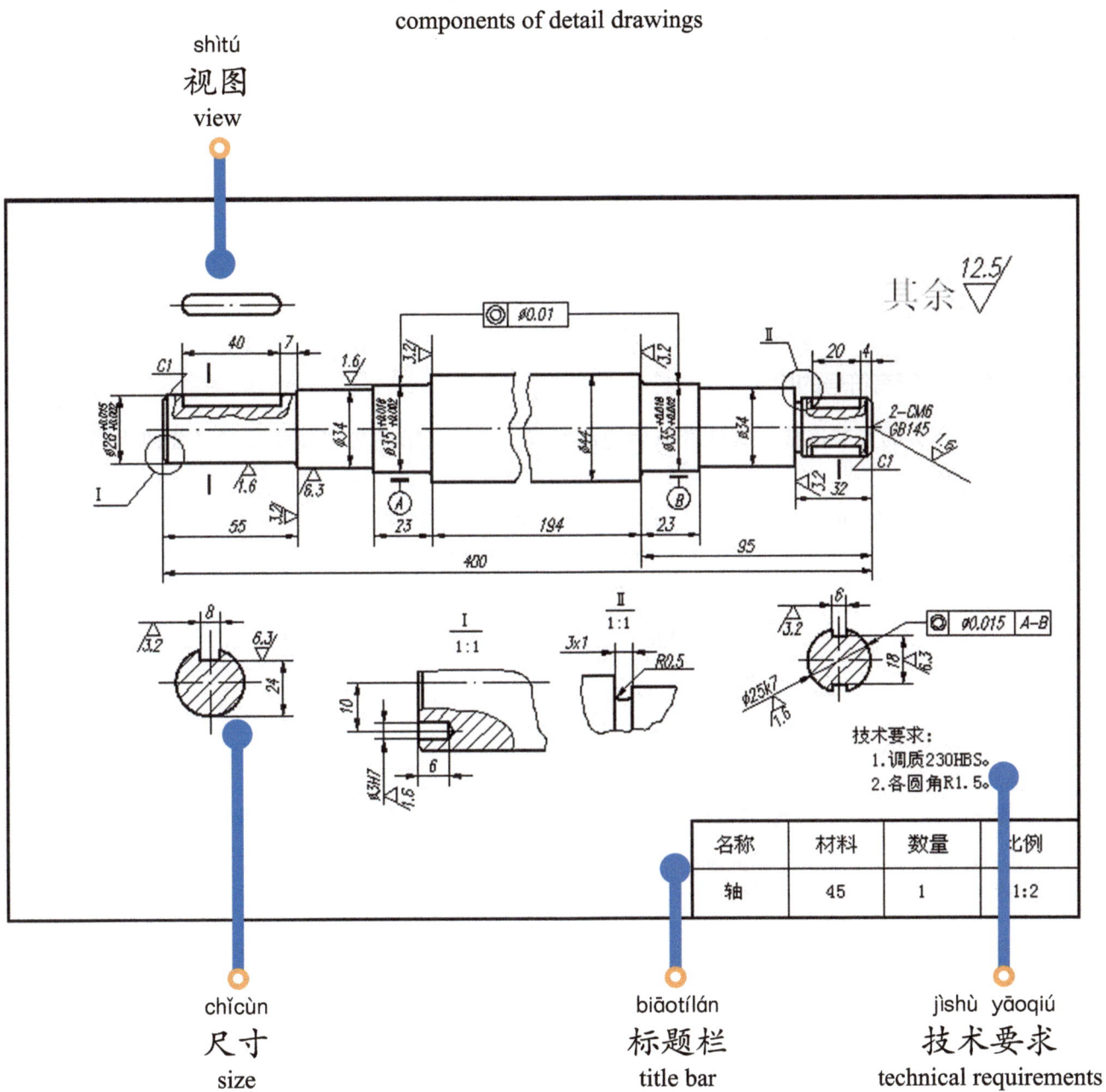

shìtú
视图
view

chǐcùn
尺寸
size

biāotílán
标题栏
title bar

jìshù yāoqiú
技术要求
technical requirements

> **题解　Introduction**
>
> 1. 学习内容：图纸的不同种类、零件图的基本组成。
>   Learning content: Different types of drawings and the basic components of a detail drawing
> 2. 知识目标：掌握隔音符号的用法，掌握与图纸相关的核心词语及表达。
>   Knowledge objectives: To master the usage of the syllable-dividing mark, and acquire the core vocabulary and expressions related to drawings
> 3. 技能目标：能识别不同的图纸。
>   Skill objective: To be able to identify different drawings

第一部分　Part 1　语音 Phonetic Learning

一、语音知识　yǔyīn zhīshi　Knowledge about Phonetics

拼写规则（5）：隔音符号的用法　Spelling rules (5): the usage of the syllable-dividing mark

a、o、e 开头的音节连接在其他音节后边的时候，如果音节的界限发生混淆，要使用隔音符号"'"隔开。例如：

When a syllable beginning with "a", "o", or "e" comes after another syllable and causes ambiguity, the syllable-dividing mark " ' " is used to distinguish the syllables. For example,

xī + ān → xiān（先）　　Xī'ān（西安）

pí + ǎo → piǎo（漂）　　pí'ǎo（皮袄）

二、语音练习　yǔyīn liànxí　Pronunciation Drills

读一读 Let's read.

① túzhǐ 图纸	② língjiàntú 零件图	③ biāotílán 标题栏	④ yì zǔ shìtú 一组视图
⑤ jìshù yāoqiú 技术要求	⑥ xíngzhuàng 形状	⑦ tèzhēng 特征	⑧ jiǎnyàn 检验
⑨ zǒngzhuāngtú 总装图	⑩ zhuāngpèi 装配	⑪ qìlùtú 气路图	⑫ diànlùtú 电路图

第二部分　Part 2
课文　Texts

一、热身　rèshēn　Warm-up

1. 给词语选择对应的图片。 Choose the corresponding picture for each word.

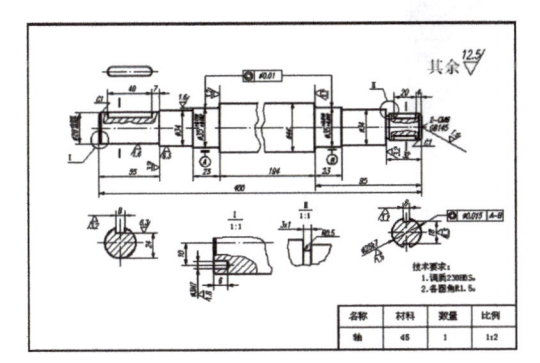

A.

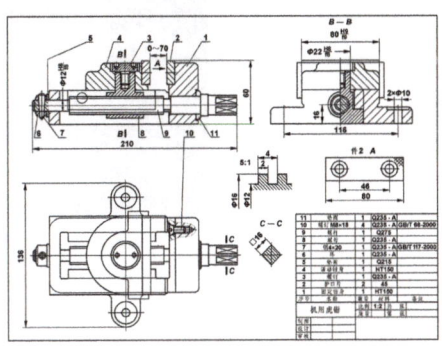

B.

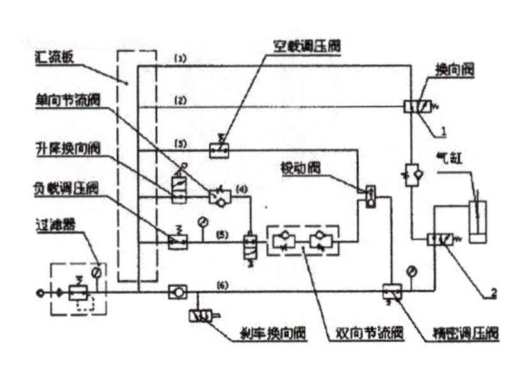

C.

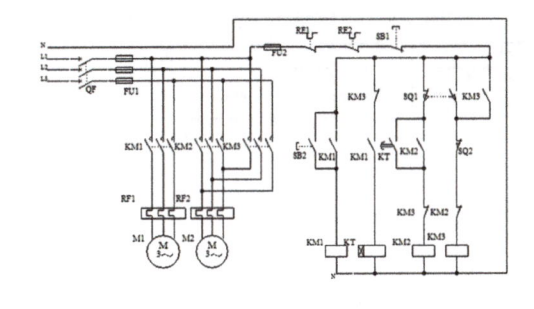

D.

① 气路图 qìlùtú _____
pneumatic circuit diagram

② 总装图 zǒngzhuāngtú _____
general assembly drawing

③ 零件图 língjiàntú _____
detail drawing

④ 电路图 diànlùtú _____
circuit diagram

2. 观看介绍零件图的主要构成的视频，将零件图主要构成部分的序号填入到合适的空格里。
Watch the video introducing the main components of detail drawings, and put the serial numbers of the main components of a detail drawing into appropriate blanks.

① biāotílán
标题栏
title bar

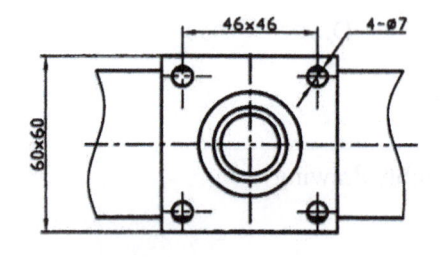

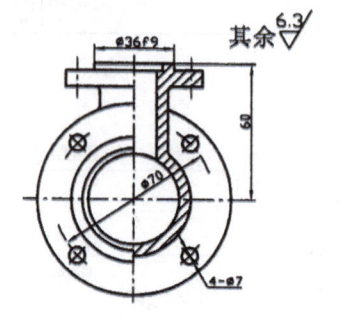

② yì zǔ shìtú
一组视图
a set of views

③ chǐcùn
尺寸
size

技术要求
1. 调质处理HB=220～240。
2. 未注倒角1×45°。
3. 未注尺寸公差按IT12。
4. 未注圆角R2。

④ jìshù yāoqiú
技术要求
technical requirements

图纸
Drawings

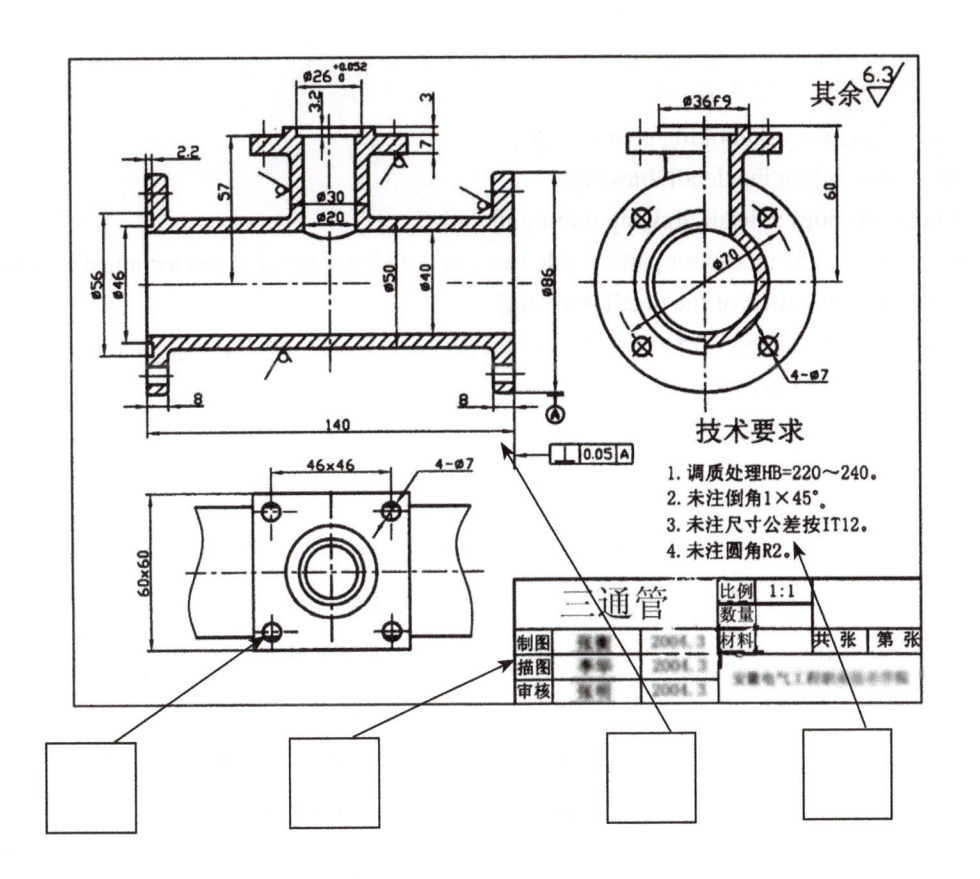

二、课文　kèwén　Texts

A　09-01

xuétú: Zhǔguǎn, nín zài kàn túzhǐ ma?
学徒：主管，您在看图纸吗？

zhǔguǎn: Shì de, wǒ zài kàn língjiàntú.
主管：是的，我在看零件图。

xuétú: Língjiàntú zhǔyào bāokuò nǎ jǐ bùfen a?
学徒：零件图主要包括哪几部分啊？

zhǔguǎn: Língjiàntú zhǔyào yóu biāotílán、yì zǔ shìtú、chǐcùn hé jìshù yāoqiú sì bùfen gòuchéng.
主管：零件图主要由标题栏、一组视图、尺寸和技术要求四部分构成。

xuétú: Língjiàntú de zuòyòng shì shénme ne?
学徒：零件图的作用是什么呢？

zhǔguǎn: Tā kěyǐ biǎoshì dāngèr língjiàn de xíngzhuàng、dàxiǎo hé tèzhēng, yě shì zài zhìzào hé jiǎnyàn jīqì língjiàn shí suǒ yòng de túyàng.
主管：它可以表示单个儿零件的形状、大小和特征，也是在制造和检验机器零件时所用的图样。

译文 yìwén Text in English

Apprentice: Supervisor, are you looking at drawings?
Supervisor: Yes, I am reading the detail drawing.
Apprentice: What parts does a detail drawing mainly include?
Supervisor: It is mainly made up of four parts: a title bar, a set of views, the size and technical requirements.
Apprentice: What is the function of the detail drawing?
Supervisor: It can show the shape, size and features of a part and is also the drawing used for manufacturing and inspecting machine parts.

普通词语 pǔtōng cíyǔ General Vocabulary 09-02

1.	在	zài	adv.	indicating an action in progress
2.	看	kàn	v.	look at, read
3.	哪	nǎ	pron.	which, what
4.	部分	bùfen	n.	part, section
5.	啊	a	part.	used at the end of a question to tone it down
6.	由	yóu	prep.	by, through
7.	四	sì	num.	four
8.	构成	gòuchéng	v.	make up, form
9.	表示	biǎoshì	v.	show
10.	单个儿	dāngèr	adj.	single
11.	所用的	suǒ yòng de	phr.	used

专业词语 zhuānyè cíyǔ Specialized Vocabulary 09-03

1.	图纸	túzhǐ	n.	drawing, blueprint
2.	零件图	língjiàntú	n.	detail drawing
	零件	língjiàn	n.	part, component
3.	标题栏	biāotílán	n.	title bar
4.	一组视图	yì zǔ shìtú	phr.	a set of views
5.	技术要求	jìshù yāoqiú	phr.	technical requirement
6.	形状	xíngzhuàng	n.	shape
7.	大小	dàxiǎo	n.	size
8.	特征	tèzhēng	n.	feature
9.	制造	zhìzào	v.	manufacture
10.	检验	jiǎnyàn	v.	inspect
11.	机器	jīqì	n.	machine
12.	图样	túyàng	n.	drawing, draft

B 09-04

学徒: 主管，这是什么图纸？
xuétú: Zhǔguǎn, zhè shì shénme túzhǐ?

主管: 这是总装图。
zhǔguǎn: Zhè shì zǒngzhuāngtú.

学徒: 总装图有什么作用呢？
xuétú: Zǒngzhuāngtú yǒu shénme zuòyòng ne?

主管: 它是用来说明机器各零部件的装配关系的。
zhǔguǎn: Tā shì yònglái shuōmíng jīqì gè língbùjiàn de zhuāngpèi guānxì de.

学徒: 除了零件图和总装图，还有其他类型的图纸吗？
xuétú: Chúle língjiàntú hé zǒngzhuāngtú, hái yǒu qítā lèixíng de túzhǐ ma?

主管: 还有气路图和电路图。
zhǔguǎn: Hái yǒu qìlùtú hé diànlùtú.

译文 yìwén Text in English

Apprentice: Supervisor, what kind of drawing is this?
Supervisor: It is a general assembly drawing.
Apprentice: What is the function of the general assembly drawing?
Supervisor: It is used to show the assembly relationship of different spare parts and components of a machine.
Apprentice: Besides detail drawings and general assembly drawings, are there other types of drawings?
Supervisor: Yes, there are pneumatic circuit diagrams and circuit diagrams.

普通词语 pǔtōng cíyǔ General Vocabulary 09-05

#	词	拼音	词性	英文
1.	说明	shuōmíng	v.	show, explain, illustrate
2.	关系	guānxì	n.	relationship
3.	除了	chúle	prep.	besides, in addition to
4.	其他	qítā	pron.	other
5.	类型	lèixíng	n.	type

专业词语 zhuānyè cíyǔ Specialized Vocabulary 09-06

#	词	拼音	词性	英文
1.	总装图	zǒngzhuāngtú	n.	general assembly drawing
2.	零部件	língbùjiàn	n.	spare parts and components
3.	装配	zhuāngpèi	v.	assemble
4.	气路图	qìlùtú	n.	pneumatic circuit diagram

5. 电路图　　　　diànlùtú　　　　n.　　　circuit diagram

三、视听说　shì-tīng-shuō　Viewing, Listening and Speaking

观看介绍零件图基本组成要素及作用的视频，然后将零件图的各组成部分与其作用相匹配。
Watch the video introducing the basic elements of detail drawings and their functions, and match the components of the detail drawing with their functions.

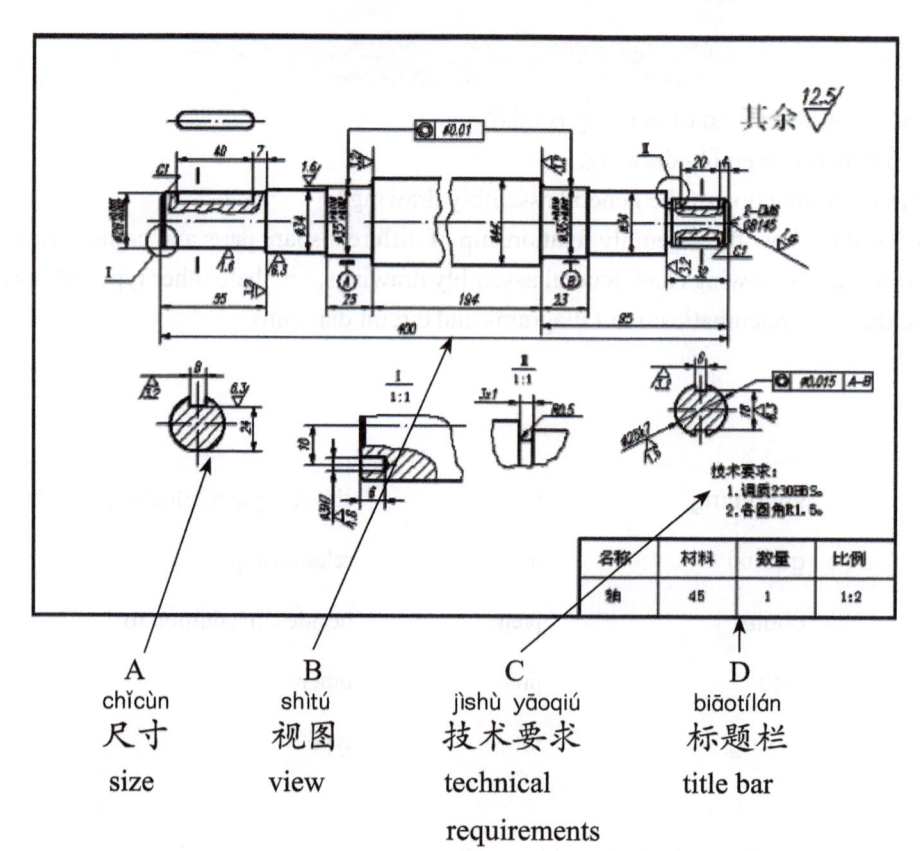

A
chǐcùn
尺寸
size

B
shìtú
视图
view

C
jìshù yāoqiú
技术要求
technical requirements

D
biāotílán
标题栏
title bar

① língjiàn xìnxī
零件信息 _____
parts information

② língjiàn dàxiǎo、wèizhi
零件大小、位置 _____
parts size and location

③ jìshù biāozhǔn
技术标准 _____
technical requirements

④ língjiàn nèiwài jiégòu
零件内外结构 _____
parts internal and external structure

四、学以致用　xuéyǐzhìyòng　Practicing What You Have Learnt

观看介绍不同类型的图纸的作用的视频，然后根据实际情况选择合适的图纸。
Watch the video introducing the functions of various types of drawings, and choose the appropriate drawings according to the actual situations.

A.

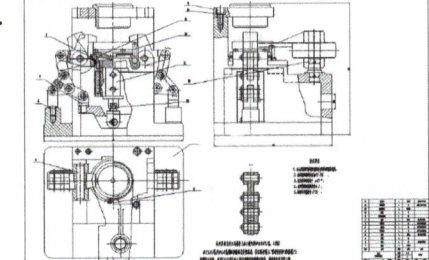

B.

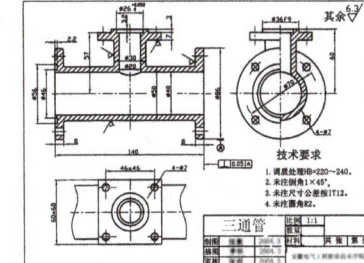

C.

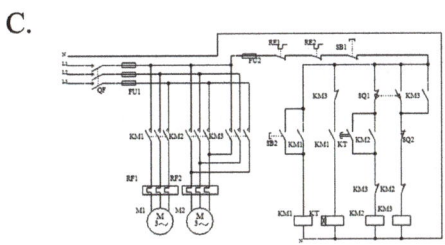

D.

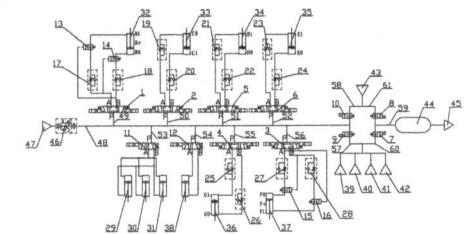

língjiàntú
❶ 零件图_____
detail drawing

zǒngzhuāngtú
❷ 总装图_____
general assembly drawing

diànlùtú
❸ 电路图_____
circuit diagram

qìlùtú
❹ 气路图_____
pneumatic circuit diagram

第三部分　Part 3　课堂用语 Classroom Expressions

❶ 你昨天怎么没来上课？　Nǐ zuótiān zěnme méi lái shàngkè? Why were you absent from class yesterday?
❷ 我期中考试没考好。　Wǒ qīzhōng kǎoshì méi kǎohǎo. I didn't do well in the mid-term exam.

第四部分　Part 4　单元实训 Unit Practical Training

认识不同的图纸
Understanding Different Drawings

实训目的 Training purpose

通过本次实训，实训人员能够认识不同图纸，了解不同图纸的作用。

Through the training, the students will be able to know different drawings and understand their functions.

实训组织 Training organization

实训人员分组，每组 4～6 人，进行图纸与名称迅速配对的活动，了解不同图纸的作用。

The students are divided into groups of 4-6. They quickly match the drawings with their names, thus understanding the functions of different drawings.

实训步骤 Training steps

❶ 教师介绍不同图纸的名称和作用。

The teacher introduces the names and functions of various drawings.

❷ 按名称找图纸：教师讲解游戏规则，宣布开始。2 名或 3 名实训人员举起有图纸名称的牌子，另 2 名或 3 名手持不同图纸的实训人员迅速找到名称配对。

Look for the drawings by the names: the teacher explains the rules of the game and kicks off the game. Two or three students hold up the cards with the names of the drawings, and the other two or three students holding different drawings match the drawings with their names quickly.

❸ 按图纸报名称：教师随机安排某名实训人员出示手中图纸，其他实训人员迅速大声地说出图纸的名称。

Speak out the names of the drawings: the teacher randomly asks a student to show the drawing in his or her hand, and other students quickly speak out the name of the drawing.

❹ 实训人员进入实习车间，教师给每个小组分发不同图纸，各小组派代表介绍图纸的作用。

The students enter the practice workshop, and the teacher hands out different drawings to each group. Each group sends a representative to introduce the function of the drawing.

❺ 教师点评，实训结束。

The teacher comments, and the training ends.

第五部分　Part 5　单元小结 Unit Summary

词语 cíyǔ Vocabulary

普通词语　General Vocabulary

1.	在	zài	adv.	indicating an action in progress
2.	看	kàn	v.	look at, read
3.	哪	nǎ	pron.	which, what
4.	部分	bùfen	n.	part, section
5.	啊	a	part.	used at the end of a question to tone it down
6.	由	yóu	prep.	by, through
7.	四	sì	num.	four
8.	构成	gòuchéng	v.	make up, form
9.	表示	biǎoshì	v.	show
10.	单个儿	dāngèr	adj.	single
11.	所用的	suǒ yòng de	phr.	used
12.	说明	shuōmíng	v.	show, explain, illustrate
13.	关系	guānxì	n.	relationship
14.	除了	chúle	prep.	besides, in addition to
15.	其他	qítā	pron.	other
16.	类型	lèixíng	n.	type

专业词语　Specialized Vocabulary

1.	图纸	túzhǐ	n.	drawing, blueprint
2.	零件图	língjiàntú	n.	detail drawing
	零件	língjiàn	n.	part, component
3.	标题栏	biāotílán	n.	title bar
4.	一组视图	yì zǔ shìtú	phr.	a set of views
5.	技术要求	jìshù yāoqiú	phr.	technical requirement
6.	形状	xíngzhuàng	n.	shape
7.	大小	dàxiǎo	n.	size
8.	特征	tèzhēng	n.	feature
9.	制造	zhìzào	v.	manufacture
10.	检验	jiǎnyàn	v.	inspect

cíyǔ 词语 Vocabulary

11.	机器	jīqì	n.	machine
12.	图样	túyàng	n.	drawing, draft
13.	总装图	zǒngzhuāngtú	n.	general assembly drawing
14.	零部件	língbùjiàn	n.	spare parts and components
15.	装配	zhuāngpèi	v.	assemble
16.	气路图	qìlùtú	n.	pneumatic circuit diagram
17.	电路图	diànlùtú	n.	circuit diagram

补充专业词语　Supplementary Specialized Vocabulary

1.	原理	yuánlǐ	n.	principle

jùzi 句子 Sentences

1. 零件图主要由标题栏、一组视图、尺寸和技术要求四部分构成。
2. 零件图可以表示单个儿零件的形状、大小和特征，也是在制造和检验机器零件时所用的图样。
3. 总装图是用来说明机器各零部件的装配关系的。
4. 除了零件图和总装图，还有气路图和电路图。

10

Cèliáng gōngjù
测量工具
Measuring Tools

cèliáng gōngjù de zhǒnglèi
测量 工具 的 种类
types of measuring tools

nèijìng qiānfēnchǐ
内径 千分尺
internal micrometer

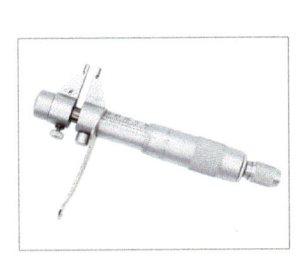

wàijìng qiānfēnchǐ
外径 千分尺
external micrometer

jiǎochǐ
角尺
angle square

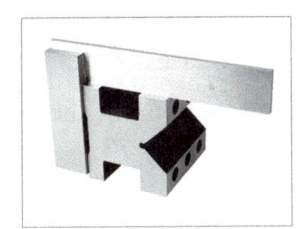

gāngzhíchǐ
钢直尺
steel gauge

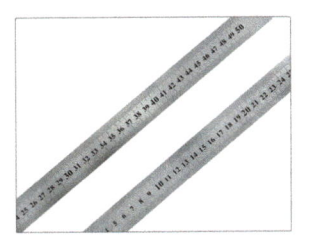

sāichǐ
塞尺
feeler gauge

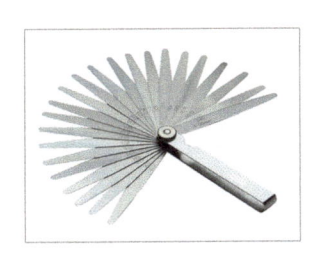

shuǐpíngyí
水平仪
level gauge

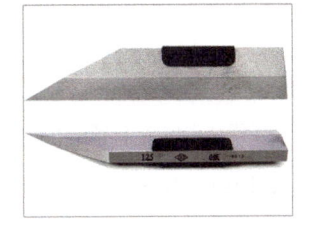

dāokǒuchǐ
刀口尺
knife straight edge

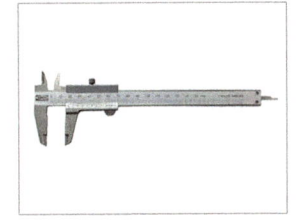

yóubiāo kǎchǐ
游标 卡尺
vernier caliper

ōumǔbiǎo
欧姆表
ohmmeter

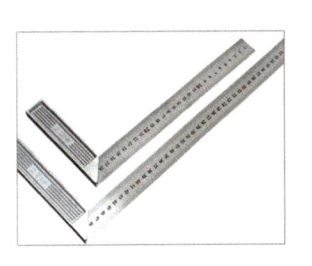

zhíjiǎochǐ
直角尺
try square

105

> **题解　Introduction**
>
> 1. 学习内容：测量工具的种类及其使用方法。
>   Learning content: The types of measuring tools and the ways of using different measuring tools
> 2. 知识目标：掌握声调标写的基本规则，掌握与测量工具相关的核心词语及表达。
>   Knowledge objectives: To master the basic rules of tone markings, and acquire the core vocabulary and expressions related to measuring tools
> 3. 技能目标：能使用不同的测量工具。
>   Skill objective: To be able to use different measuring tools

第一部分　Part 1　语音 Phonetic Learning

一、语音知识　yǔyīn zhīshi　Knowledge about Phonetics

声调的标写　Marking of tones

声调标写在一个音节的主要元音上，按照 a、o、e、i、u、ü 的先后顺序标调。韵母 iu、ui 的声调标在后一个元音上，声调标在 i 上面时，i 上的小点要省去。例如：

The tone mark is written above the main vowel of a syllable. The tone is marked according to the following order: "a", "o", "e", "i", "u", "ü". The exception is in the cases of "iu" and "ui", when the tone mark is written above the latter vowel. When the tone mark is placed on "i", the dot on the top of "i" is omitted. For example,

dà	mén	duō	lèi	xué	shuǐ	niú	xīn
大	门	多	累	学	水	牛	心

二、语音练习　yǔyīn liànxí　Pronunciation Drills

读一读　Let's read.

1. cèliáng gōngjù　测量工具
2. dāokǒuchǐ　刀口尺
3. zhíxiàndù　直线度
4. yóubiāo kǎchǐ　游标卡尺
5. ōumǔbiǎo　欧姆表
6. diànyā　电压
7. diànliú　电流
8. jiǎochǐ　角尺
9. nèijìng qiānfēnchǐ　内径千分尺
10. wàijìng qiānfēnchǐ　外径千分尺
11. shuǐpíngyí　水平仪
12. sāichǐ　塞尺

第二部分 Part 2

课文 Texts

一、热身 rèshēn Warm-up

1. 给词语选择对应的图片。Choose the corresponding picture for each word.

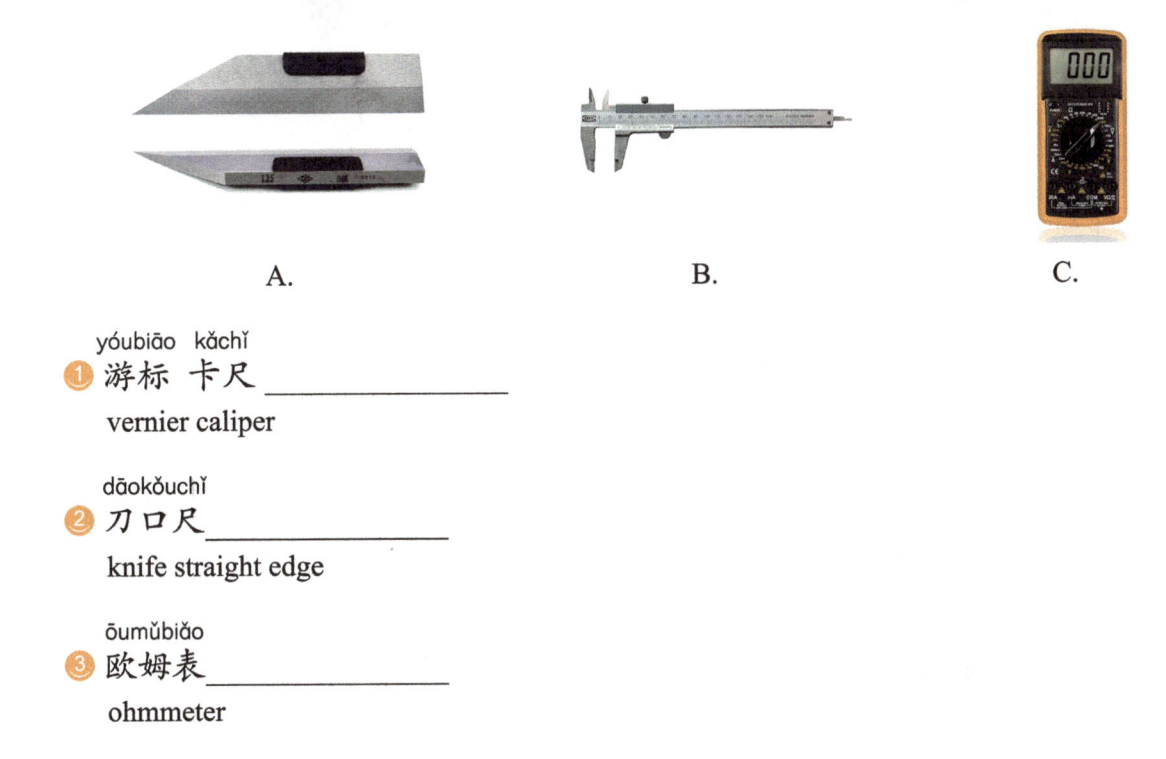

A.　　　　　　　　　B.　　　　　　　　　C.

① yóubiāo kǎchǐ
游标 卡尺 _____
vernier caliper

② dāokǒuchǐ
刀口尺 _____
knife straight edge

③ ōumǔbiǎo
欧姆表 _____
ohmmeter

2. 观看介绍测量工具的视频，将测量工具的序号填入到合适的空格里。Watch the video introducing measuring tools, and put the serial numbers of the tools into the appropriate blanks.

rènshi cèliáng gōngjù
认识 测量 工具
understand measuring tools

中文+机电一体化（初级）

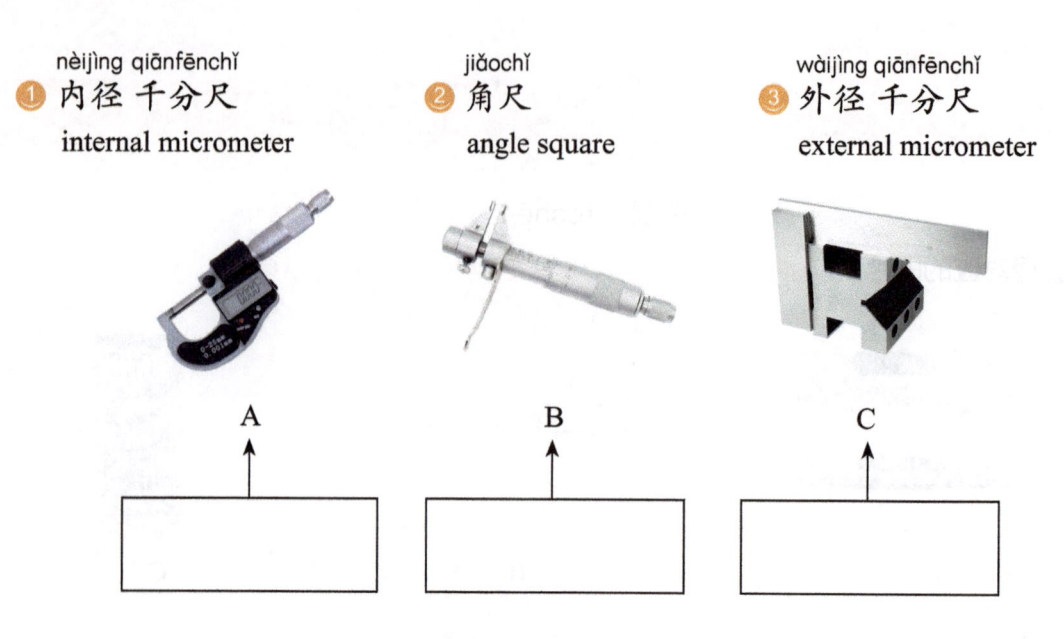

① nèijìng qiānfēnchǐ
内径 千分尺
internal micrometer

② jiǎochǐ
角尺
angle square

③ wàijìng qiānfēnchǐ
外径 千分尺
external micrometer

A B C

二、课文　kèwén　Texts

A 10-01

xuétú: Zhǔguǎn, qǐngwèn xìnxī jiǎnsuǒ zhōngxīn zài nǎr?
学徒：主管，请问信息检索中心在哪儿？

zhǔguǎn: Chūle chējiānmén yòu guǎi, yìzhí zǒu, zǒuláng jìntóu de nà jiān jiù shì.
主管：出了车间门右拐，一直走，走廊尽头的那间就是。

xuétú: Xièxie! Wǒmen zěnyàng jiǎncè gōngjiàn shìfǒu hégé ne?
学徒：谢谢！我们怎样检测工件是否合格呢？

zhǔguǎn: Wǒmen shǐyòng cèliáng gōngjù jìnxíng jiǎncè.
主管：我们使用测量工具进行检测。

xuétú: Dāokǒuchǐ shì yònglái jiǎncè zhíxiàndù de ma?
学徒：刀口尺是用来检测直线度的吗？

zhǔguǎn: Shì de, yóubiāo kǎchǐ shì yònglái cèliáng chǐcùn de.
主管：是的，游标卡尺是用来测量尺寸的。

译文 yìwén Text in English

Apprentice: Supervisor, could you tell me where the information retrieval center is?
Supervisor: Turn right after you go out of the workshop and go straight ahead. It is the one at the end of the corridor.
Apprentice: Thank you! How do we check whether the workpiece is qualified or not?
Supervisor: We use measuring tools to check.
Apprentice: Is a knife straight edge used for testing straightness?
Supervisor: Yes, and the vernier caliper is used to measure size.

测量工具
Measuring Tools 10

普通词语 pǔtōng cíyǔ General Vocabulary 🎧 10-02

1.	中心	zhōngxīn	n.	center
2.	哪儿	nǎr	pron.	where
3.	出	chū	v.	go out
4.	门	mén	n.	door
5.	右	yòu	n.	right
6.	拐	guǎi	v.	turn, change direction
7.	一直	yìzhí	adv.	straight
8.	走	zǒu	v.	walk
9.	走廊	zǒuláng	n.	corridor, porch
10.	尽头	jìntóu	n.	end
11.	那	nà	pron.	that
12.	间	jiān	m.	*a measure word used of smallest units of housing*
13.	怎样	zěnyàng	pron.	how
14.	是否	shìfǒu	adv.	if, whether

专业词语 zhuānyè cíyǔ Specialized Vocabulary 🎧 10-03

1.	检索	jiǎnsuǒ	v.	search, retrieve
2.	检测	jiǎncè	v.	test and determine, monitor and check
3.	合格	hégé	adj.	qualified
4.	测量工具	cèliáng gōngjù	phr.	measuring tool
	测量	cèliáng	v.	measure
5.	刀口尺	dāokǒuchǐ	n.	knife straight edge
6.	直线度	zhíxiàndù	n.	straightness
7.	游标卡尺	yóubiāo kǎchǐ	phr.	vernier caliper

B 🎧 10-04

xuétú: Zhǔguǎn, zhè shì shénme cèliáng gōngjù?
学徒：主管，这是什么测量工具？

zhǔguǎn: Zhè shì ōumǔbiǎo, kěyǐ cèliáng diànyā hé diànliú.
主管：这是欧姆表，可以测量电压和电流。

xuétú: Nàge shì jiǎochǐ ma?
学徒：那个是角尺吗？

zhǔguǎn: Shì de, jiǎochǐ kěyǐ jiǎnchá gōngjiàn de chuízhídù. Hái yǒu nèijìng qiānfēnchǐ hé
主管：是的，角尺可以检查工件的垂直度。还有内径千分尺和

wàijìng qiānfēnchǐ, tāmen kěyǐ cèliáng gōngjiàn nèijìng hé wàijìng de chǐcùn.
外径千分尺，它们可以测量工件内径和外径的尺寸。

译文 yìwén Text in English

Apprentice: Supervisor, what measuring tool is this?
Supervisor: It's an ohmmeter which can measure voltage and electrical current.
Apprentice: Is that an angle square?
Supervisor: Yes. It can check the perpendicularity of the workpiece. Internal micrometer and external micrometer are also included, they can measure the sizes of the internal diameter and external diameter of the workpiece.

普通词语 pǔtōng cíyǔ General Vocabulary 🎧 10-05

| 1. | 那个 | nàge | pron. | that |

专业词语 zhuānyè cíyǔ Specialized Vocabulary 🎧 10-06

1.	欧姆表	ōumǔbiǎo	n.	ohmmeter
2.	电压	diànyā	n.	voltage
3.	电流	diànliú	n.	electrical current
4.	角尺	jiǎochǐ	n.	angle square
5.	垂直度	chuízhídù	n.	perpendicularity, verticality
6.	内径千分尺	nèijìng qiānfēnchǐ	phr.	internal micrometer
	内径	nèijìng	n.	internal diameter
7.	外径千分尺	wàijìng qiānfēnchǐ	phr.	external micrometer
	外径	wàijìng	n.	external diameter

110

三、视听说　shì-tīng-shuō　Viewing, Listening and Speaking

观看介绍测量工具的种类和作用的视频，根据不同的特点选择合适的测量工具，并模仿说出工具名称及作用。Watch the video introducing the types and functions of measuring tools, choose the appropriate tools based on different characteristics, and tell the names and functions of the tools.

① shuǐpíngyí
水平仪
level gauge

② sāichǐ
塞尺
feeler gauge

③ luóxuán cèwēiqì
螺旋测微器
micrometer screw gauge

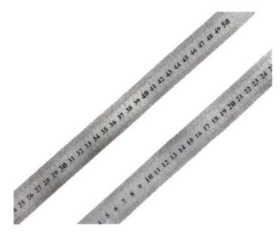

④ gāngzhíchǐ
钢直尺
steel gauge

A. cèliáng jīběn chángdù
测量基本长度 _____
measuring basic length

B. cèliáng jiānjù
测量间距 _____
measuring spacing

C. jiǎnyàn shuǐpíng wèizhi
检验水平位置 _____
testing horizontal position

D. jīngmì cèliáng chángdù
精密测量长度 _____
measuring length with high precision

四、学以致用　xuéyǐzhìyòng　Practicing What You Have Learnt

观看介绍测量工具的作用的视频，根据实际情况选择合适的测量工具。Watch the video introducing the functions of measuring tools, and choose the appropriate measuring tools according to the actual situations.

cèliáng gōngjù de zuòyòng
测量工具的作用
functions of measuring tools

ōumǔbiǎo
A. 欧姆表
ohmmeter

yóubiāo kǎchǐ
B. 游标卡尺
vernier caliper

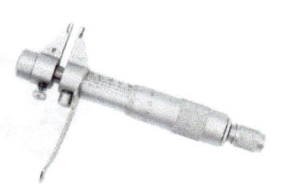

nèijìng qiānfēnchǐ
C. 内径千分尺
internal micrometer

dāokǒuchǐ
D. 刀口尺
knife straight edge

wàijìng qiānfēnchǐ
E. 外径千分尺
external micrometer

jiǎochǐ
F. 角尺
angle square

cèliáng chǐcùn
❶ 测量尺寸_____
measuring the size

cèliáng nèijìng chǐcùn
❷ 测量内径尺寸_____
measuring the internal diameter

jiǎncè zhíxiàndù
❸ 检测直线度_____
testing the straightness

cèliáng wàijìng chǐcùn
❹ 测量外径尺寸_____
measuring the external diameter

jiǎnchá gōngjiàn de chuízhídù
❺ 检查工件的垂直度_____
measuring the perpendicularity of a workpiece

cèliáng diànyā hé diànliú
❻ 测量电压和电流_____
measuring the voltage and electrical current

第三部分　Part 3　课堂用语 Classroom Expressions

❶ 十点上课，请大家准时到。Shí diǎn shàngkè, qǐng dàjiā zhǔnshí dào. We will meet at 10 o'clock. Please be on time.

❷ 现在听写。Xiànzài tīngxiě. Now it's time for dictation.

第四部分　Part 4　单元实训 Unit Practical Training

测量工具的识读
Recognition of Measuring Tools

实训目的 Training purpose

通过本次实训，实训人员能够认识测量工具并掌握其使用方法。

Through the training, the students will be able to know measuring tools and their uses.

实训组织 Training organization

实训人员分组，每组 4～6 人，小组内进行图片与工具迅速配对活动以及工具的实际操作练习。

The students are divided into groups of 4-6. Each group quickly matches the pictures with the tools and has hands-on practice of the tools.

实训步骤 Training steps

❶ 教师讲解游戏规则，宣布根据图片找工具活动开始。

The teacher explains the rules of the game and announces the activity of finding tools based on the pictures starts.

❷ 2 名或 3 名实训人员举起工具名称的图片，另 2 名或 3 名实训人员迅速找到相应的工具。

Two or three students hold up the pictures with the names of measuring tool, and the other two or three students quickly find the corresponding tools.

❸ 教师讲解测量工具的使用方法。

The teacher explains the uses of measuring tools.

❹ 实训人员在工作车间进行测量工具的实际操作。

The students use the measuring tools in the workshop.

❺ 教师示范讲解并点评，实训结束。

The teacher makes a demonstration and comments, and the training ends.

单元小结 Unit Summary

普通词语 General Vocabulary

1.	中心	zhōngxīn	n.	center
2.	哪儿	nǎr	pron.	where
3.	出	chū	v.	go out
4.	门	mén	n.	door
5.	右	yòu	n.	right
6.	拐	guǎi	v.	turn, change direction
7.	一直	yìzhí	adv.	straight
8.	走	zǒu	v.	walk
9.	走廊	zǒuláng	n.	corridor, porch
10.	尽头	jìntóu	n.	end
11.	那	nà	pron.	that
12.	间	jiān	m.	a measure word used of smallest units of housing
13.	怎样	zěnyàng	pron.	how
14.	是否	shìfǒu	adv.	if, whether
15.	那个	nàge	pron.	that

cíyǔ 词语 Vocabulary

专业词语 Specialized Vocabulary

1.	检索	jiǎnsuǒ	v.	search, retrieve
2.	检测	jiǎncè	v.	test and determine, monitor and check
3.	合格	hégé	adj.	qualified
4.	测量工具	cèliáng gōngjù	phr.	measuring tool
	测量	cèliáng	v.	measure
5.	刀口尺	dāokǒuchǐ	n.	knife straight edge
6.	直线度	zhíxiàndù	n.	straightness
7.	游标卡尺	yóubiāo kǎchǐ	phr.	vernier caliper
8.	欧姆表	ōumǔbiǎo	n.	ohmmeter
9.	电压	diànyā	n.	voltage
10.	电流	diànliú	n.	electrical current

cíyǔ 词语 Vocabulary

11.	角尺	jiǎochǐ	n.	angle square
12.	垂直度	chuízhídù	n.	perpendicularity, verticality
13.	内径千分尺	nèijìng qiānfēnchǐ	phr.	internal micrometer
	内径	nèijìng	n.	internal diameter
14.	外径千分尺	wàijìng qiānfēnchǐ	phr.	external micrometer
	外径	wàijìng	n.	external diameter

补充专业词语　Supplementary Specialized Vocabulary

1.	水平仪	shuǐpíngyí	n.	level meter
2.	塞尺	sāichǐ	n.	feeler gauge
3.	螺旋测微器	luóxuán cèwēiqì	phr.	micrometer screw gauge
4.	钢直尺	gāngzhíchǐ	n.	steel gauge

jùzi 句子 Sentences

1. 信息检索中心在哪儿？出了车间门右拐，一直走，走廊尽头的那间就是。
2. 刀口尺是用来检测直线度的。
3. 游标卡尺是用来测量尺寸的。
4. 欧姆表可以测量电压和电流。
5. 角尺可以检查工件的垂直度。
6. 内径千分尺和外径千分尺可以测量工件内径和外径的尺寸。

附录 Appendixes

词汇总表 Vocabulary

序号	生词	拼音	词性	词义	普通 G/专业 S	所属单元
1	啊	a	part.	used at the end of a question to tone it down	G	9A
2	安排	ānpái	n./v.	arrangement; arrange	G	6A
3	安全	ānquán	adj.	safe	S	3A
4	安全	ānquán		SECURITY	S	5
5	安全标志	ānquán biāozhì	phr.	safety sign	S	4A
6	安全帽	ānquánmào	n.	safety helmet	S	3B
7	安全通道	ānquán tōngdào	phr.	safe passage	S	4A
8	安全鞋	ānquánxié	n.	safety shoes	S	3B
9	安全眼镜	ānquán yǎnjìng	phr.	safety goggles	S	3B
10	安装	ānzhuāng	v.	install	S	1A
11	按	àn	prep.	according to	G	3B
12	按照	ànzhào	prep.	according to	G	8A
13	把	bǎ	prep.	used to put the object before the verb	G	5B
14	白底	bái dǐ	phr.	white background	S	4
15	扳手	bānshou	n.	wrench	S	6
16	板锉	bǎncuò	n.	flat file	S	7B
17	包含	bāohán	v.	include	G	4B
18	包括	bāokuò	v.	include	G	1A
19	保障	bǎozhàng	v.	protect, ensure	S	3A
20	比如	bǐrú	v.	such as, for example	G	5B
21	边框	biānkuàng	n.	frame	S	4
22	标题栏	biāotílán	n.	title bar	S	9A
23	标志	biāozhì	n.	sign	S	4A
24	表达	biǎodá	v.	express	G	4B
25	表面	biǎomiàn	n.	surface	G	7A
26	表示	biǎoshì	v.	show	G	9A
27	部分	bùfen	n.	part, section	G	9A
28	操作	cāozuò	v.	operate	G	8A
29	操作工	cāozuògōng	n.	operator	S	2A
30	测量	cèliáng	v.	measure	S	10A

（续表）

序号	生词	拼音	词性	词义	普通 G/专业 S	所属单元
31	测量工具	cèliáng gōngjù	phr.	measuring tool	S	10A
32	车床	chēchuáng	n.	lathe	S	2
33	车工	chēgōng	n.	lathe operator	S	2
34	车间	chējiān	n.	workshop	S	1A
35	尺寸	chǐcùn	n.	size	G	8A
36	出	chū	v.	go out	G	10A
37	除了	chúle	prep.	besides, in addition to	G	9B
38	触电	chù//diàn	v.	get an electric shock	S	4
39	穿	chuān	v.	put on, wear	S	3A
40	穿戴	chuāndài	v.	wear	S	3A
41	传感器	chuángǎnqì	n.	sensor	S	1
42	垂直度	chuízhídù	n.	perpendicularity, verticality	S	10B
43	从	cóng	prep.	from	G	7A
44	存储	cúnchǔ	v.	store	S	6B
45	锉	cuò	v.	make smooth with a file	S	7A
46	锉刷	cuòshuā	n.	file brush	S	7
47	锉削	cuòxiāo	v.	file	S	7A
48	打扫	dǎsǎo	v.	sweep, clean	S	5A
49	大家	dàjiā	pron.	everybody, everyone	G	3B
50	大小	dàxiǎo	n.	size	S	9A
51	代表	dàibiǎo	v.	represent, stand for	G	4A
52	戴	dài	v.	wear (a hat, a mask, etc.)	S	3A
53	单个儿	dāngèr	adj.	single	G	9A
54	当心	dāngxīn	v.	watch out	S	4
55	刀口尺	dāokǒuchǐ	n.	knife straight edge	S	10A
56	到	dào	v.	used as a complement of a verb indicating the result of an action	G	5B
57	倒	dào	v.	dump, pour	G	5A
58	倒垃圾	dào lājī	phr.	take out the trash	G	5A
59	的	de	part.	used after an attribute when it modifies a noun in the usual way	G	1B
60	等	děng	part.	etc., and so on	G	4B
61	地面	dìmiàn	n.	floor	S	5A

（续表）

序号	生词	拼音	词性	词义	普通G/专业S	所属单元
62	电工	diàngōng	n.	electrician	S	2A
63	电流	diànliú	n.	electrical current	S	10B
64	电路图	diànlùtú	n.	circuit diagram	S	9B
65	电气	diànqì	n.	electricity, electric power	S	1A
66	电压	diànyā	n.	voltage	S	10B
67	掉	diào	v.	used after some verbs to indicate the result of an action	G	7A
68	动手	dòng//shǒu	v.	do, get to work	G	8A
69	堆放	duīfàng	v.	pile	S	5
70	多余	duōyú	adj.	excess, redundant, superfluous	G	7A
71	耳塞	ěrsāi	n.	earplug	S	3
72	方法	fāngfǎ	n.	method, way	G	5B
73	方面	fāngmiàn	n.	field, aspect, side	G	1A
74	防尘口罩	fángchén kǒuzhào	phr.	dust mask	S	3
75	防护	fánghù	v.	protect	S	3A
76	放	fàng	v.	put, place	G	5B
77	负责	fùzé	v.	be responsible for, account for	G	1B
78	干净	gānjìng	adj.	clean	S	5A
79	钢卷尺	gāngjuǎnchǐ	n.	steel tape measure	S	6A
80	钢直尺	gāngzhíchǐ	n.	steel gauge	S	10
81	高度尺	gāodùchǐ	n.	height gauge	S	8
82	高压电	gāoyādiàn	n.	high-voltage electricity	S	4
83	个	gè	m.	a measure word usually used before a noun having no particular classifier	G	1A
84	个人	gèrén	n.	person, individual	S	3A
85	各	gè	pron.	all, every	G	6B
86	各种	gèzhǒng	pron.	various, all kinds of	G	6B
87	工件	gōngjiàn	n.	workpiece	S	7A
88	工具	gōngjù	n.	tool	S	6A
89	工具柜	gōngjùguì	n.	tool cabinet	S	6B
90	工具箱	gōngjùxiāng	n.	tool kit	S	2
91	工作	gōngzuò	n.	work, job	G	1B
92	工作服	gōngzuòfú	n.	work clothes	S	3B

119

(续表)

序号	生词	拼音	词性	词义	普通 G/专业 S	所属单元
93	工作台	gōngzuòtái	n.	workbench	S	6B
94	构成	gòuchéng	v.	make up, form	G	9A
95	拐	guǎi	v.	turn, change direction	G	10A
96	关系	guānxì	n.	relationship	G	9B
97	管理	guǎnlǐ	v.	manage	S	5B
98	还	hái	adv.	also, as well	G	3A
99	焊接面罩	hànjiē miànzhào	phr.	welding mask	S	3
100	好	hǎo	adj.	good, fine	G	1A
101	好的	hǎo de	phr.	all right	G	3B
102	号	hào	n.	number	G	3A
103	号	hào	m.	(usually used after numerals) an ordinal number for a date of a month	G	7A
104	号码	hàomǎ	n.	number	G	3A
105	合格	hégé	adj.	qualified	S	10A
106	和	hé	conj.	and	G	1B
107	黑色	hēisè	n.	black	S	4
108	很	hěn	adv.	very, so	G	5A
109	横杠	héng gàng	phr.	horizontal bar	S	4
110	红色	hóngsè	n.	red	S	4
111	后	hòu	n.	(of time) (in) future, later time	G	3B
112	划规	huàguī	n.	scribing compass	S	8
113	划线	huà//xiàn	v.	mark lines	S	8A
114	画	huà	v.	draw, paint	G	8A
115	环境	huánjìng	n.	environment	S	5A
116	黄色	huángsè	n.	yellow	S	4
117	货架	huòjià	n.	goods shelves	S	5A
118	机电	jīdiàn	n.	electromechanical equipment	S	1A
119	机电一体化	jīdiàn yītǐhuà	phr.	mechatronics	S	1A
120	机器	jīqì	n.	machine	S	9A
121	机器人	jīqìrén	n.	robot	S	1
122	机械	jīxiè	n.	machinery, mechanisms	S	1A
123	机械装置	jīxiè zhuāngzhì	phr.	mechanical device	S	1

(续表)

序号	生词	拼音	词性	词义	普通G/专业S	所属单元
124	几	jǐ	pron.	how many, what	G	7A
125	计算机	jìsuànjī	n.	computer	S	1A
126	计算机技术	jìsuànjī jìshù	phr.	computer technology	S	1A
127	技术	jìshù	n.	technology, technique	S	1A
128	技术要求	jìshù yāoqiú	phr.	technical requirement	S	9A
129	加	jiā	v.	add	G	3A
130	间	jiān	m.	a measure word used of smallest units of housing	G	10A
131	检测	jiǎncè	v.	test and determine, monitor and check	S	10A
132	检查	jiǎnchá	v.	check	S	5A
133	检索	jiǎnsuǒ	v.	search, retrieve	S	10A
134	检验	jiǎnyàn	v.	inspect	S	9A
135	减少	jiǎnshǎo	v.	reduce	S	3A
136	教	jiāo	v.	teach	G	3B
137	角尺	jiǎochǐ	n.	angle square	S	10B
138	叫	jiào	v.	name, call	G	2A
139	接线	jiē//xiàn	v.	connect a cable, wire	S	2
140	今天	jīntiān	n.	today	G	3B
141	金属	jīnshǔ	n.	metal	S	7A
142	尽头	jìntóu	n.	end	G	10A
143	进行	jìnxíng	v.	conduct	G	5A
144	进入	jìnrù	v.	enter	G	3B
145	禁止	jìnzhǐ	v.	prohibit	S	4B
146	禁止标志	jìnzhǐ biāozhì	phr.	prohibition sign	S	4B
147	警告	jǐnggào	v.	warn	S	4B
148	警告标志	jǐnggào biāozhì	phr.	warning sign	S	4B
149	救护	jiùhù	v.	give first-aid (to)	S	4B
150	救护标志	jiùhù biāozhì	phr.	first-aid sign	S	4B
151	就	jiù	adv.	at once, right away	G	5A
152	锯	jù	v.	saw	S	8A
153	锯割	jùgē	v.	saw	S	8
154	锯弓	jùgōng	n.	saw bow	S	6A

中文+机电一体化（初级）

（续表）

序号	生词	拼音	词性	词义	普通 G/专业 S	所属单元
155	锯条	jùtiáo	n.	saw blade	S	8B
156	锯削	jùxiāo	v.	saw	S	8A
157	开	kāi	v.	open	G	8A
158	看	kàn	v.	look at, read	G	9A
159	靠铁	kàotiě	n.	cast iron angle plate	S	8
160	可以	kěyǐ	aux.	may, can	G	3A
161	库房	kùfáng	n.	warehouse	S	3B
162	垃圾	lājī	n.	garbage, trash	G	5A
163	垃圾桶	lājītǒng	n.	trash can	S	5
164	来	lái	v.	do (*used a substitute for a more specific verb. e.g., to bring or to have*)	G	8A
165	劳保	láobǎo	n.	labor protection	S	3A
166	了	le	part.	*used at the end of a sentence to indicate a change or the emergence of a new situation*	G	5A
167	了	le	part.	*used after a verb/an adjective to indicate the completion of an action/a change*	G	5B
168	类型	lèixíng	n.	type	G	9B
169	李明	Lǐ Míng	pn.	a person's name	G	2A
170	里	li	n.	the state of being in/inside	G	2A
171	零部件	língbùjiàn	n.	spare parts and components	S	9B
172	零件	língjiàn	n.	part, component	S	9A
173	零件图	língjiàntú	n.	detail drawing	S	9A
174	六月	liùyuè	n.	June	G	7A
175	螺帽	luómào	n.	nut	S	6
176	螺栓	luóshuān	n.	screw bolt	S	6
177	螺丝刀	luósīdāo	n.	screwdriver	S	6
178	螺旋测微器	luóxuán cèwēiqì	phr.	micrometer screw gauge	S	10
179	绿色	lǜsè	n.	green	G	4A
180	吗	ma	part.	*used at the end of a question*	G	5B
181	忙	máng	adj.	busy	G	5A
182	毛刺	máocì	n.	burr	S	7B
183	门	mén	n.	door	G	10A
184	名字	míngzi	n.	name	G	2A

（续表）

序号	生词	拼音	词性	词义	普通G/专业S	所属单元
185	哪	nǎ	pron.	which, what	G	9A
186	哪儿	nǎr	pron.	where	G	10A
187	哪些	nǎxiē	pron.	which, who, what	G	1A
188	那	nà	conj.	then, in that case	G	4A
189	那	nà	pron.	that	G	10A
190	那个	nàge	pron.	that	G	10B
191	呢	ne	part.	*used at the end of a question*	G	2B
192	内径	nèijìng	n.	internal diameter	S	10B
193	内径千分尺	nèijìng qiānfēnchǐ	phr.	internal micrometer	S	10B
194	内容	nèiróng	n.	content	G	1A
195	能源	néngyuán	n.	energy	S	1
196	你	nǐ	pron.	you (*singular*)	G	1A
197	你好	nǐ hǎo	phr.	hello, how do you do	G	1A
198	你们	nǐmen	pron.	you (*plural*)	G	1A
199	您	nín	pron.	you (*honorific*)	G	2A
200	欧姆表	ōumǔbiǎo	n.	ohmmeter	S	10B
201	拍照	pāi//zhào	v.	take a picture	S	4
202	培训	péixùn	v.	train	S	5B
203	平台	píngtái	n.	platform	S	6B
204	期间	qījiān	n.	period, course	G	3B
205	其他	qítā	pron.	other	G	9B
206	气路图	qìlùtú	n.	pneumatic circuit diagram	S	9B
207	前	qián	n.	(in time) the past, the time before	G	5B
208	钳工	qiángōng	n.	fitter	S	2A
209	钳工锤	qiángōngchuí	n.	fitter's hammer	S	6A
210	清洁	qīngjié		SEIKETSU	S	5
211	清洁工具	qīngjié gōngjù	phr.	cleaning tool	S	5
212	清扫	qīngsǎo		SEISO	S	5
213	请	qǐng	v.	please	G	1A
214	请问	qǐngwèn	v.	may I ask	G	1A
215	区域	qūyù	n.	area	S	5B
216	去	qù	v.	go	G	3B

123

(续表)

序号	生词	拼音	词性	词义	普通G/专业S	所属单元
217	去除	qùchú	v.	remove, get rid of	S	7B
218	然后	ránhòu	conj.	then, afterwards	G	8A
219	任务	rènwu	n.	task	G	8A
220	如果	rúguǒ	conj.	if	G	3A
221	如何	rúhé	pron.	how	G	3B
222	塞尺	sāichǐ	n.	feeler gauge	S	10
223	三	sān	num.	three	G	1A
224	三角锉刀	sānjiǎo cuòdāo	phr.	triangular file	S	7B
225	三角形	sānjiǎoxíng	n.	triangle	S	4
226	扫地	sǎo//dì	v.	sweep the floor	S	5B
227	上班	shàng//bān	v.	work	S	3A
228	上	shang	n.	used after a noun to indicate the scope of sth	G	1B
229	设备	shèbèi	n.	equipment	S	1A
230	什么	shénme	pron.	used in the interrogative before a noun to ask about people/things	G	2A
231	生产	shēngchǎn	v.	produce	S	1A
232	生产线	shēngchǎnxiàn	n.	production line	S	1A
233	时	shí	n.	time	G	3A
234	使用	shǐyòng	v.	use	G	6B
235	事故	shìgù	n.	accident	S	3A
236	试	shì	v.	test, try	S	2B
237	试运转	shì yùnzhuǎn	phr.	test run	S	2B
238	是	shì	v.	be	G	3A
239	是否	shìfǒu	adv.	if, whether	G	10A
240	手机	shǒujī	n.	mobile phone	G	3A
241	手钳	shǒuqián	n.	plier	S	6
242	手套	shǒutào	n.	gloves	S	3
243	水平仪	shuǐpíngyí	n.	level meter	S	10
244	说明	shuōmíng	v.	show, explain, illustrate	G	9B
245	四	sì	num.	four	G	9A
246	素养	sùyǎng		SHITSUKE	S	5
247	所用的	suǒ yòng de	phr.	used	G	9A

（续表）

序号	生词	拼音	词性	词义	普通 G/专业 S	所属单元
248	它	tā	pron.	it	G	4A
249	它们	tāmen	pron.	they, them	G	3A
250	台虎钳	táihǔqián	n.	bench vice	S	6A
251	特定	tèdìng	adj.	specific	S	4B
252	特征	tèzhēng	n.	feature	S	9A
253	调整	tiáozhěng	v.	adjust	S	2B
254	调整工	tiáozhěnggōng	n.	tool setter	S	2A
255	贴标签	tiē biāoqiān	phr.	attach labels	S	5
256	铁屑	tiěxiè	n.	iron filings	S	7
257	通道	tōngdào	n.	passage, passageway access	S	4A
258	图样	túyàng	n.	drawing, draft	S	9A
259	图纸	túzhǐ	n.	drawing, blueprint	S	9A
260	外径	wàijìng	n.	external diameter	S	10B
261	外径千分尺	wàijìng qiānfēnchǐ	phr.	external micrometer	S	10B
262	完成	wán//chéng	v.	complete	G	5B
263	万用表	wànyòngbiǎo	n.	multimeter	S	2
264	王伟	Wáng Wěi	pn.	a person's name	G	2A
265	微信	wēixìn	n.	WeChat	G	3A
266	为什么	wèi shénme	pron.	why, for what reason	G	3A
267	维修	wéixiū	v.	maintain	S	1A
268	问	wèn	v.	ask, inquire	G	1A
269	问题	wèntí	n.	question, problem	G	3A
270	我	wǒ	pron.	I, me	G	2A
271	我们	wǒmen	pron.	we, us	G	5A
272	物品	wùpǐn	n.	article, product	S	5B
273	吸烟	xī//yān	v.	smoke	S	4
274	铣床	xǐchuáng	n.	milling machine	S	2
275	铣工	xǐgōng	n.	miller	S	2
276	喜欢	xǐhuan	v.	like	G	8A
277	现在	xiànzài	n.	now	G	5B
278	线	xiàn	n.	line	G	8A
279	削	xiāo	v.	pare with a knife, whittle	S	7A

（续表）

序号	生词	拼音	词性	词义	普通G/专业S	所属单元
280	信息	xìnxī	n.	information	S	4B
281	星期一	xīngqīyī	n.	Monday	G	7A
282	形状	xíngzhuàng	n.	shape	S	9A
283	需要	xūyào	v.	need	G	7B
284	旋出	xuánchū	phr.	screw out	S	6
285	旋入	xuánrù	phr.	screw in	S	6
286	学徒	xuétú	n.	apprentice	S	1A
287	学习	xuéxí	v.	study, learn	G	5B
288	呀	ya	part.	a variant of 啊 used after a word ending in a, e, i, o or ü	G	4A
289	沿着	yánzhe	phr.	along	G	8A
290	颜色	yánsè	n.	color	G	4A
291	眼镜	yǎnjìng	n.	glasses, spectacles	S	3B
292	要求	yāoqiú	n./v.	requirement; require	G	3B
293	要	yào	aux.	should, have to	G	2B
294	也	yě	adv.	also, too	G	3A
295	一	yī	num.	one	G	4A
296	一般	yìbān	adj.	general, usual	G	1A
297	一体化	yìtǐhuà	v.	integrate	S	1A
298	一些	yìxiē	q.	some	G	3A
299	一直	yìzhí	adv.	straight	G	10A
300	一组视图	yì zǔ shìtú	phr.	a set of views	S	9A
301	意思	yìsi	n.	meaning	G	4A
302	应该	yīnggāi	aux.	should	G	5B
303	用来	yònglái	phr.	use	G	4B
304	用品	yòngpǐn	n.	articles for use	S	3A
305	由	yóu	prep.	by, through	G	9A
306	游标卡尺	yóubiāo kǎchǐ	phr.	vernier caliper	S	10A
307	有	yǒu	v.	there is, exist	G	2A
308	右	yòu	n.	right	G	10A
309	预防	yùfáng	v.	take precautions against, prevent	S	3A
310	原理	yuánlǐ	n.	principle	S	9

(续表)

序号	生词	拼音	词性	词义	普通G/专业S	所属单元
311	圆锉刀	yuán cuòdāo	phr.	round file	S	7B
312	圆形	yuánxíng	n.	round, circle	S	4
313	月	yuè	n.	month	G	7A
314	运转	yùnzhuǎn	v.	run, operate	S	2B
315	在	zài	prep.	used to indicate time, scope, place, condition, etc.	G	3B
316	在	zài	adv.	indicating an action in progress	G	9A
317	怎么	zěnme	pron.	how	G	8B
318	怎样	zěnyàng	pron.	how	G	10A
319	这	zhè	pron.	this	G	4A
320	这里	zhèlǐ	pron.	here	G	4A
321	这样	zhèyàng	pron.	this	G	3A
322	整顿	zhěngdùn		SEITON	S	5
323	整洁	zhěngjié	adj.	clean and tidy, neat	S	5A
324	整理	zhěnglǐ	v.	arrange, tidy up	S	5A
325	整理	zhěnglǐ		SEIRI	S	5
326	执行装置	zhíxíng zhuāngzhì	phr.	actuator	S	1
327	直线度	zhíxiàndù	n.	straightness	S	10A
328	指定	zhǐdìng	v.	designate	S	5B
329	指示	zhǐshì	v.	indicate	S	4B
330	指示标志	zhǐshì biāozhì	phr.	direction sign	S	4B
331	制造	zhìzào	v.	manufacture	S	9A
332	置物架	zhìwùjià	n.	commodity shelf	S	5
333	中心	zhōngxīn	n.	center	G	10A
334	种	zhǒng	m.	kind, type	G	5B
335	种类	zhǒnglèi	n.	kind, type	G	2A
336	主管	zhǔguǎn	n.	supervisor	S	1A
337	主要	zhǔyào	adj.	main, major	G	1B
338	装配	zhuāngpèi	v.	assemble	S	9B
339	总装图	zǒngzhuāngtú	n.	general assembly drawing	S	9B
340	走	zǒu	v.	walk	G	10A
341	走廊	zǒuláng	n.	corridor, porch	G	10A

127

（续表）

序号	生词	拼音	词性	词义	普通G/专业S	所属单元
342	昨天	zuótiān	n.	yesterday	G	5B
343	作用	zuòyòng	n.	function	G	7B
344	做	zuò	v.	do	G	2B

视频脚本　Video Scripts

第一单元　机电一体化概述

一、热身
A：机电一体化公司的工作环境是怎样的？
B：机电一体化公司的工作环境一般包括生产车间、自动化生产线、维修车间、仓库、会议室。

三、视听说
A：机器人由哪些装置构成？
B：由机械装置、执行装置、能源、传感器和计算机五个部分构成。机械装置，是机器人的手指、手臂、手臂的连接部分和机座。执行装置，是使机器人动起来的电气装置。能源，提供电源和动力。传感器，监视机器人的运动。计算机，计算和判断机器人的运动。

四、学以致用
大家好！今天我来给大家说说生活中有哪些机电一体化产品，例如：复印机、打印机、扫描仪等办公设备，以及空调、洗衣机、冰箱等家用电器，还有照相机、电脑、平板电脑、手机等电子产品。这些都是机电一体化产品。

第二单元　机电专业岗位

一、热身
A：电工在做什么？
B：电工在接线。
A：钳工要做什么？
B：钳工要划线、锉削和锯削。
A：维修工要干什么？
B：维修工要维修各类设备。

三、视听说
A：机电一体化公司有哪些工作岗位？
B：在机电一体化公司里，职位最高的是总经理，在他之下，有生产经理和销售经理。生产经理之下又有三个主管：生产主管、维修主管和机加主管。

四、学以致用
操作车床的工人，称为车工。操作铣床的工人，称为铣工。电气维修工，使用万用表对电气设备进行检测。机械维修工使用扳手、螺丝刀、钳子等工具进行修理。

第三单元　车间安全培训

一、热身
A：在生产和维修时，我们要穿戴哪些劳保用品？
B：我们要戴帽子，保护头部。戴安全眼镜，保护眼睛。穿工作服并且戴上手套，保护皮肤。穿安全鞋，保护脚。有时我们还要戴防尘口罩，防止吸入灰尘。

三、视听说
A：什么时候要戴安全帽？

B：在高于两米作业和有空中坠物危险时要戴安全帽。
A：安全帽怎么佩戴？
B：先检查外观，如果有损坏及时报废。戴上安全帽后，系紧下颚带，调节后箍，防止脱落。女员工如果是长发，要将长发盘起，放到安全帽内。不能将安全帽提在手里，也不能在安全帽里面或者外面戴其他帽子。

四、学以致用

大家好！今天我来给大家介绍机电设备安全操作的规程。
（1）清除不必要物件，保证来去畅通；
（2）正确穿戴好劳保用品；
（3）检查机电设备的各个部件和防护装置；
（4）设备运转时，操作者不能离开，应细心观察；
（5）工作结束切断电源；
（6）清理工具，清扫设备。

第四单元　安全标志

一、热身

A：你好！安全工程师，墙上的图片是什么？
B：你好！那是安全标志。这些警告标志是黄黑三角形，表示见到图示物质必须特别小心；白底圆形的，有红色边框和红色横杠的是禁止标志，表示应禁止的行为。

三、视听说

A：这是什么标志？
B：这是警告标志，表示此处有高压电。
A：那是什么标志？
B：那是号令标志，表示必须戴安全帽。
A：这些是什么标志？
B：这些是救护标志，表示这是安全通道。
A：那些是什么标志？
B：那些是禁止标志，表示那些地方不许拍照。

四、学以致用

大家好！今天我来给大家说说不同场景应张贴的不同安全标志。在仓库里，我们会看到禁止吸烟的禁止标志；在厂区道路上，会看到小心叉车的警告标志；在生产车间，会张贴小心触电的标志；在操作台上，有当心夹手的标志。这些不同的标志都告诉我们一件非常重要的事情，那就是注意安全。

第五单元　6S 管理

一、热身

A：仓库作业现场处理需要做什么？
B：出入库单据整理归档，现场卫生打扫干净，货品排放整齐，搬运工具、叉车摆放到规定区域，安全检查等。

三、视听说

A：组长，为什么要开展 6S 管理呀？
B：为了有一个干净的工作环境，遵守规定，提高管理水平。
A：6S 管理包括哪些活动呢？
B：6S 管理即整理、整顿、清扫、清洁、素养、安全。

四、学以致用

大家好！今天我来给大家说说6S管理中的整顿，请您学会整顿。机器设备要定期保养，贴上设备保养卡；工具和零部件要定位放置，有统一标识；车间各区域要有6S责任区和责任人。

第六单元　钳工工具

一、热身

A：这是什么？
B：这是螺丝刀，用来旋入或旋出螺丝。
A：那是什么？
B：那是扳手，用来旋入或旋出螺栓或螺帽。
A：这个呢？
B：这是手钳，主要夹持材料或工件。

三、视听说

A：大家认识一下钳工设备，这是六角钳工台，用于安装台虎钳。台虎钳是夹持工件的通用夹具。这是砂轮机，用于磨削各种工具或刀具。
B：好的，我认识了这些钳工设备。

四、学以致用

大家好！今天我来给大家说说不同场景需要用到的钳工工具。这是样冲，划线时需要的；这是手锤，錾削时要用到的；这是锉削用的锉刀；这是孔加工时需要的麻花钻；这是刮削时使用的平面刮刀。

第七单元　锉削

一、热身

A：首先，我们夹紧工件，然后用板锉去除工件表面的毛刺，最后再用锉刷刷去工件表面的铁屑。
B：好的，我来学做一遍。

三、视听说

A：我们先确认图纸，然后确定工件毛坯，接着检查毛坯尺寸，现在开始加工，完成加工后进行测量，最后确定成品与图纸是否相符。这样我们就完成了锉削的过程。
B：好的，明白了。

四、学以致用

大家好！今天我来给大家说说不同工件类型所需要的不同锉削工具：首先，对于中间有三角形孔的工件，我们选用三角锉；普通工件要用板锉；圆形孔我们用圆形锉。

第八单元　划线与锯削

一、热身

A：组长，请问锯削的基本步骤是什么？
B：锯削主要分为三步：首先用靠铁固定工件，接着用高度尺划线，最后用锯弓锯条锯割工件。

三、视听说

A：划线的主要步骤是：第一步用靠铁固定工件，第二步将高度尺调到准确高度，最后一步用划规划线。
B：好的，我来操作一遍。

四、学以致用

大家好！今天我来给大家说说划线和锯削过程中工具的作用。划线平台是划线的操作平台，靠铁用来固定工件，高度尺用来调节准确高度，划规用来划线，锯弓用来锯割工件。

第九单元　图纸

一、热身
A：零件图是由哪几部分构成的？
B：零件图主要由标题栏、视图、尺寸和技术要求四部分构成。

三、视听说
A：零件图是由哪几部分构成的？
B：零件图主要由标题栏、视图、尺寸和技术要求四部分构成。
A：那每个部分的作用是什么？
B：标题栏注明与零件相关的信息，视图表达零件的内外结构，尺寸确定零件各部分的大小和位置，技术要求是指零件在技术方面应该达到的要求。

四、学以致用
大家好！今天我来给大家说说不同类型图纸的作用。零件图表示单个零件形状、大小和特征；总装图说明机器的装配关系；气路图显示机器零部件的气路原理；电路图显示机器零部件的电路原理。

第十单元　测量工具

一、热身
A：这是什么测量工具？
B：这是内径千分尺，那是外径千分尺。另一个有角度的是角尺。

三、视听说
A：我们经常使用的测量工具有哪些啊？
B：常用的有钢直尺、塞尺、水平仪、螺旋测微仪（一般我们称千分尺）等。
A：那它们的主要作用是什么呢？
B：钢直尺是基本的长度量具，塞尺主要用于间隙间距的测量，水平仪主要检验设备安装的水平位置，螺旋测微仪（千分尺）是非常精密的长度测量工具。

四、学以致用
大家好！今天我来给大家说说各种测量工具的作用。刀口尺用来检测直线度，游标卡尺可以测量尺寸，欧姆表测量电压和电流，内径千分尺和外径千分尺用来测量内径和外径的尺寸，直角尺可以检查工件的垂直度。

参考答案　Reference Answers

第一单元

一、热身

1. ①A　②D　③B　④C
2.

A → C → D → E → B

三、视听说

①B　②A　③D　④C

四、学以致用

①√　②√　③√　④√　⑤√　⑥×　⑦×　⑧√

第二单元

一、热身

1. ①B　②D　③A　④C
2. ①D　②A、B、C　③E

三、视听说

```
        zǒngjīnglǐ
          总经理
     general manger
      /          \
shēngchǎn jīnglǐ   ④
   生产 经理
production manager
   /    |    \
  ③    ②    ①
```

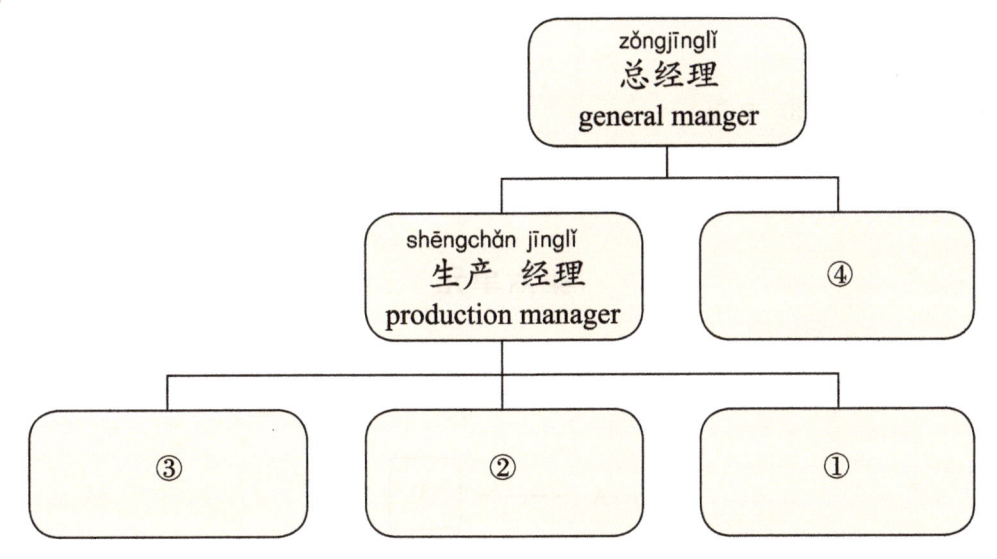

四、学以致用

①C　②A　③B　④D

第三单元

一、热身

1. ①C　②A　③D　④B
2. ①B　②A　③D　④C　⑤E

133

三、视听说

①√ ②× ③× ④× ⑤× ⑥×

四、学以致用

C → B → E → A → D → F

第四单元

一、热身

1. ①D ②A ③B ④C

2. ①A、C ②B、D

三、视听说

②，③，④，①

四、学以致用

①—D ②—A ③—B ④—C

第五单元

一、热身

1. ①A ②D ③C ④B

2.

③ → ② → ① → ⑤ → ④

三、视听说

A① B④ C⑥ D② E③ F⑤

四、学以致用

①—C ②—D ③—A ④—B

第六单元

一、热身

1. ①B ②C ③D ④A

2.

A → ③

B → ②

C → ①

三、视听说
①C　②B　③A

四、学以致用
①C　②D　③B　④E　⑤A

第七单元

一、热身
1. ①B　②D　③A　④C
2. ②　①　③

三、视听说

②→③→①→④→⑥→⑤

四、学以致用
①—C　②—A　③—B

第八单元

一、热身
1. ①D　②B　③A　④C
2.

②→①→③

三、视听说
②　①　③

四、学以致用
①E　②C　③B　④D　⑤A

第九单元

一、热身
1. ①C　②B　③A　④D
2.

③→①→②→④

三、视听说
①D　②A　③C　④B

四、学以致用
①B　②A　③C　④D

第十单元

一、热身
1. ① B ② A ③ C
2.

A → ③

B → ①

C → ②

三、视听说
A. ④ B. ② C. ① D. ③

四、学以致用
① B ② C ③ D ④ E ⑤ F ⑥ A